T0294177

TREKKING IN GREENLAND

TREKKING IN GREENLAND

THE ARCTIC CIRCLE TRAIL
by Paddy Dillon

JUNIPER HOUSE, MURLEY MOSS,
OXENHOLME ROAD, KENDAL, CUMBRIA LA9 7RL
www.cicerone.co.uk

© Paddy Dillon 2019
Second edition 2019
ISBN: 978 1 85284 967 2
Reprinted 2022, 2023 (with updates)
First edition 2010

Printed in Turkey by Pelikan Basim on responsibly sourced paper.

A catalogue record for this book is available from the British Library.

All photographs are by the author unless otherwise stated.

All route maps © Visit Greenland. Copies of the printed maps from which these extracts are taken are available from Visit Greenland, Postboks 1615, Hans Egedesvej 29, 3900 Nuuk, Tel: (+299) 34 28 20, info@visitgreenland.com, www.visitgreenland.com.

Updates to this Guide

While every effort is made by our authors to ensure the accuracy of guidebooks as they go to print, changes can occur during the lifetime of an edition. Any updates that we know of for this guide will be on the Cicerone website (www.cicerone.co.uk/967/updates), so please check before planning your trip. We also advise that you check information about such things as transport, accommodation and shops locally. Even rights of way can be altered over time. We are always grateful for information about any discrepancies between a guidebook and the facts on the ground, sent by email to updates@cicerone.co.uk or by post to Cicerone, Juniper House, Murley Moss, Oxenholme Road, Kendal LA9 7RL.

Register your book: To sign up to receive free updates, special offers and GPX files where available, register your book at www.cicerone.co.uk.

Front cover: Trekkers take a break before descending to Kangerluatsiarsuaq (Day 4)

CONTENTS

Warning

Walking across remote Arctic tundra can be a dangerous activity carrying a risk of personal injury or death. It should be undertaken only by those with a full understanding of the risks, and with the training and experience to evaluate them. While every care and effort has been taken in the preparation of this guide, the user should be aware that weather conditions and the level of water in rivers can be highly variable and can change quickly, materially affecting the seriousness of this trek. Therefore, except for any liability which cannot be excluded by law, they cannot accept responsibility for any loss, injury or inconvenience sustained by any person using this book.

For mountain/wilderness rescue in Greenland, the first point of contact is the police. Ring Sisimiut, 70 13 22, or 70 14 48 in the evenings; or Kangerlussuaq, tel 70 13 24, or 70 14 48 in the evenings.

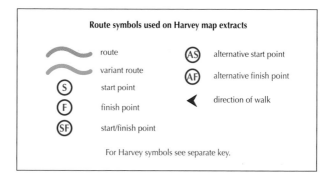

Route symbols used on Harvey map extracts

~~	route	(AS)	alternative start point
~~	variant route	(AF)	alternative finish point
(S)	start point		
(F)	finish point	◄	direction of walk
(SF)	start/finish point		

For Harvey symbols see separate key.

Polar view of Greenland

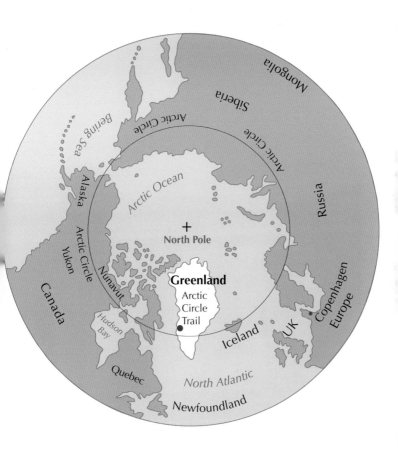

A lake beyond Iluliumanersuup Portornga on the way to Innajuattoq (Day 6)

Crossing the river at the start of Day 7

INTRODUCTION

The scenery along the Arctic Circle Trail looks like an uninhabited version of the Scottish Highlands

Greenland is the largest island on Earth, excluding the continental landmasses, with an area of 2,175,600km² (840,000 square miles). Greenland is also one of the world's most inhospitable and sparsely populated places, with an ice cap occupying 85 per cent of the landmass, leaving only a narrow coastal strip ice-free during the summer. The bulk of Greenland lies north of the Arctic Circle – the line of latitude 66° 33' 39". In high summer this is the 'Land of the Midnight Sun', but in the deepest midwinter there is no sun at all, just the eerie flickering of the northern lights.

Greenland is a harsh environment, where every type of life has had to adapt to survive the long and bitterly cold winter. It is also a fascinating place to explore, especially on foot in remote places, and in the summer months it can be surprisingly easy. Geographically, Greenland is part of the North American continent, but politically it is tied to Denmark and Europe. The country was granted home rule as recently as 21 June 2009.

The Arctic Circle Trail is a splendid trekking route that fits neatly into one of the largest ice-free areas of West Greenland, lying 40–50km (25–30 miles) north of the Arctic Circle. The trail runs 165km (103 miles) between Kangerlussuaq and Sisimiut, and the total ascent/descent along the route is surprisingly low, at 4105m (13,465ft). Walkers usually take 7–10 days to complete the route.

It is estimated that around 1300 people per year walk the trail, maybe many more, arriving from all parts of the world. They are usually experienced backpackers, but this is often their first experience of walking in Greenland. Access to the trail is easy, and the walk can commence immediately from the international airport at Kangerlussuaq. Although Greenland has the reputation of being an expensive place to travel, the Arctic Circle Trail is completely free of charge. The trail is equipped with a series of basic huts, for which there is no charge, and it costs nothing to pitch a tent in the wilds. At one point there is the option of paddling a canoe along a lake – again free of charge. Some walkers even fish or gather berries along the trail to supplement their rations!

Well-prepared walkers, who take care to pack lightweight and efficient gear, will doubtless rank the Arctic Circle Trail as one of the classic walks of the world. There is an incredible sense of open space from start to finish, and, if blessed with sunny and stable weather, few walkers would wish to be anywhere else. It is essentially a summer route, and this guidebook describes the trail during the brief summer months (June to September), when the tundra is vibrant with new life. The dark Arctic winter, with its

sub-zero temperatures, is of course a completely different experience!

This guidebook describes the trail as it existed up until 2018. Please note that there is a plan to convert part of the trail into a dirt road, and if this plan ever comes to fruition, expect to find quarries, bulldozers and other intrusive works. This plan might never come to pass, but it might also be your last chance to enjoy this remarkable trail.

GEOLOGY

Greenland is part of the Laurentian Shield. This is a vast area of ancient rock, among the oldest exposed rock in the world, stretching across much of North America. Whatever its original structure, it has been altered beyond recognition during the course of its existence as it was crushed under incredible pressures, causing it to melt and re-crystallise over and over again. Vast areas of rock were torn apart, crumpled together and intruded by a variety of igneous rocks and mineral veins. Unravelling the long and complex history of Greenland's geology is time-consuming, but geological study is made much simpler because so much of the bedrock is buried out of sight (and hence out of mind) beneath the ice cap, or beneath glacial drift and blanket bog.

In the region of the Arctic Circle Trail the bedrock is broadly described as being Palaeoprotozoic (2500 to 1600 million years old) and Archaean (as much as 3800 million years old).

During that distant epoch the Earth's atmosphere was high in methane and ammonia. The earliest life forms were stromatolites, anaerobic cyanobacteria which very slowly enriched the oxygen content of the air, making it possible for more complex life forms to evolve.

The rocks around Kangerlussuaq are part of the Ikertoq Complex, formed of Archaean gneiss. This metamorphic rock has been substantially altered over time. It contains a large number of 'kimberlite' and 'lamproite' dykes, roughly trending north-west to south-east. While geologists might argue about precise definitions, these dykes are attracting the attention of diamond prospectors. Don't expect anyone to lead you to any diamonds, though there are tours to Garnet Mountain, where you can chip for lesser gemstones.

The Archaean gneiss has been thrust northwards, and the Arctic Circle Trail passes through the thrust zone at its halfway stage, where the geology becomes even more complex, passing a formation described as a 'syntectonic granite suite'. Towards the end of the trail around Sisimiut, the bedrock is Palaeoprotozoic, a mere 1900 million years old. These rocks belong to the Isortoq Complex, and are mainly granitic and metamorphic charnockite.

Billions of years of Greenland's geological history are completely missing from the Arctic Circle Trail, but are represented in other parts of the country. Over that expanse of time, Greenland was part of the super-continent of Pangaea. As such, the country's landmass has been situated at the

Gneiss is a highly variable metamorphic rock which often exhibits intense folding and mineral veins

Equator, submerged beneath the sea, risen from the sea and been trodden by dinosaurs. Around 100 million years ago Greenland parted company with Europe and drifted westwards as part of the North American continent. Only in relatively recent geological time has Greenland become the ice-bound Arctic island seen today.

Fossiliferous rocks are completely absent along the Arctic Circle Trail. However, shortly after leaving Kangerlussuaq, the route climbs above a coastal site called Fossilsletten, where relatively recent post-glacial fossilised marine shells are contained in thick beds of sand and clay. In some low-lying valleys along the trail, similar marine deposits are found, dating only from the end of the Ice Age.

A comprehensive and colourful book, full of useful and interesting information, available in English, but too heavy to carry on the trail, is the Geological History of Greenland, by Niels Henriksen, published by the Geological Survey of Denmark and Greenland (GEUS).

THE ICE CAP

Around 85 per cent of Greenland is still in the grip of the Ice Age, covered by a vast ice cap (Danish – inlandsisen) that reaches a maximum thickness of about 3km (2 miles) in the middle of the country. In some places the ice reaches the sea, where it 'calves' icebergs into the water. In other places the ice terminates more than 200km (125 miles) from the sea, leaving a strip of land that is free of snow and ice throughout the summer. The Arctic Circle Trail exploits one of the widest of these ice-free

The savage coast of eastern Greenland, where glaciers push their way straight into the ocean

regions, which enjoys some of the country's best weather.

Ice is apparently solid and brittle, but under stress it can bend, becoming plastic, with the ability to melt and re-freeze almost imperceptibly. This allows the entire ice sheet to 'flow' inexorably downwards and outwards from the centre of Greenland towards the edges. The fastest rate of 'flow' is around 20m (65ft) per day, but at the same time, the edges of the ice sheet are melting. This melting causes an apparent 'retreat' during the summer, followed by an apparent 'advance' during the winter. In fact, the ice is advancing all the time, but with climate change it is melting back at a far greater rate than ever recorded before.

For those undertaking the Arctic Trail, the easiest way to visit the ice cap is from Kangerlussuaq, where four-wheel drive vehicles follow a dirt road north-east past Russells Glacier to a place known as 'Point 660'. Visitors can stroll around on the edge of the ice cap, and the journey there and back can be accomplished in an afternoon. No other part of Greenland's ice cap is so easily accessible, so make the most of it while in the area. Beware of crumbling rubble moraine at the edge of the ice, and keep away from torrential, murky glacial rivers. Not only do these rivers flow fast and furiously, but the sand and mud-banks near them are notoriously unstable.

It's worth remembering that the fringes of Greenland aren't as ice-free as they might appear. If you were to dig deep into the thick beds of mud, sand and gravel in some places, you would discover frozen ground and even big chunks of stagnant ice. This permanently frozen ground is called 'permafrost', and like the ice cap and glaciers, it is gradually melting. When big chunks of ice melt inside thick layers of sediment the ground caves in, forming deep water-filled holes called 'pingos'. Countless thousands of little pools dotted around the edges of Greenland were formed in this manner.

The underlying geology of the Arctic Circle Trail, and its recent scouring by glaciers, has created in a rather bleak landscape. Nearby mountains peak between 1000m and 1500m (3280ft and 4920ft), while the valleys between them are seldom higher than 300m (985ft), and often much less. The Arctic Circle Trail only rarely reaches an altitude of 450m (1475ft). There is abundant bare rock, but also thick deposits of gravel, sand and mud. Some places are well vegetated, while in others vegetation is sparse. In permanently wet areas the vegetation cannot decay completely, and forms thick layers of peat that become blanket bog. Overall, the scenery is reminiscent of how the Scottish Highlands must have looked before anyone lived there!

A Greenland sled pup wants nothing more than to grow big and strong and pull a sled in winter

WILDLIFE

A summer trek along the Arctic Circle Trail reveals abundant wildlife, despite the species count being low. It could be described as 'big game' country, with reindeer (*Rangifer tarandus*) and musk ox (*Ovibus moshatus*) likely to be seen. Greenlanders, unlike their distant cousins the Sami of Finland, hunt reindeer, rather than herd them. Reindeer antlers and bones are seen on a daily basis on the trail. Juvenile reindeer are inquisitive and may approach walkers, while adults are quick to flee. Stocky, shaggy musk ox, related to sheep and goats, were hunted almost to the point of extinction, but the area around Kangerlussuaq was restocked in the 1960s with 27 calves, and their numbers are now around 8000 strong. Musk ox are only rarely seen on the trail. By all means admire them, but give them

wide berth. They are unpredictable, especially in family groups, and might charge anyone approaching them.

Mighty polar bears (*Ursus maritimus*) shouldn't be seen, as there is no reason for them to be in the area, but there have been a couple of recent unexpected sightings near Kangerlussuaq. Humble lemmings (*Discrostonyx torquatus*) aren't present, as the Arctic Circle Trail isn't part of their range. Two animals that do occasionally make an appearance are the arctic hare (*Lepus arcticus*) and arctic fox (*Alopex lagopus*). The hare is white, as are some of the foxes, but other foxes are a dark colour, referred to as 'blue'.

Although not 'wild', Greenland sled dogs are not exactly 'tame' either. Forbidden to live in the towns, sled dogs are generally tethered en masse somewhere out of earshot. Only a few of these dogs live at Kangerlussuaq, though more are brought into the area in winter. At Sisimiut, walkers pass many sled dogs as they walk to and from town, and the former campsite is now overrun by them. When one dog starts howling, they all start howling like wolves!

Land mammals are few in number, but a trip to sea from Sisimiut could reveal a variety of whales, seals and possibly even a walrus. The sea contains a number of fish species, including cod, halibut, redfish and wolf fish. It is worth visiting the Qimatulivik shop in Sisimiut to inspect the 'catch of the day'. Inland, clear lakes and rivers contain arctic char and salmon, which some walkers attempt to catch to supplement their food rations. (Note that a fishing licence is required, obtainable from the police, although in practice

they may tell you not to bother applying!) Notable birds include a variety of small species that dart, flutter and twitter among the Arctic scrub. Look out for the northern wheatear (*Oenanthe oenanthe*), common redpoll (*Acanthis flammea*) and snow bunting (*Plectrophenax nivalis*). The well-camouflaged ptarmigan (*Lagopus mutus*) will tolerate a close approach. They are rather like grouse in size and habit. Black ravens (*Corvus corax*) are spotted on a daily basis, while birds of prey include the peregrine falcon (*Falco peregrinus*) and gyrfalcon (*Falco rusticolus*). Gyrfalcon nests near Kangerlussuaq have been used almost every summer for 2500 years! With luck, a white-tailed eagle (*Haliaetus albicilla*) might be seen.

The abundant lakes support ducks, geese, waders and wildfowl. The largest lakes are home to the red-throated loon (*Gavia stellata*),

Reindeer can be seen almost every day along the Arctic Circle Trail, and will tolerate a close approach

which often laughs at passing walkers and canoeists, or sometimes pipes a lament to their suffering! Canada geese (*Branta canadensis*) and mallards (*Anas platyrhynchos*) are commonly seen, along with a variety of gulls near the coast. Sometimes, a cormorant (*Phalacrocorax carbo*) will wing its way inland.

Insect life is abundant in high summer, but while butterflies may delight the eye, nothing causes more misery than the mosquitoes and biting flies. From mid-June throughout July they can be a plague, but their numbers are vastly depleted towards the end of August, and by September they may be absent altogether. Consider using insect repellent and head nets in June and July, and hope that the first frosts decimate the mosquitoes soon afterwards.

There is little available in English covering Greenland's wildlife apart from *A Nature and Wildlife Guide to Greenland* by Benny Génsbøl, published by Gyldendal. The pictures in some books may prove helpful. Try *Grønlands Dyr og Planter*, by Benny Génsbøl and Carl Christian Tofte, published by Gads Forlag.

PLANTS AND FLOWERS

Four main plant species occur in varying densities from one end of the Arctic Circle Trail to the other, so it is worth being able to identify them at the earliest opportunity, especially those with food value! Greenland is

18

often said to be treeless, but in fact is it covered in trees – vast forests of miniature trees. The northern willow (*Salix glauca*) is often a creeping shrub, but can grow to 2–3m (6–10ft) in sheltered locations, and is one of the most common plants in Greenland. The dwarf birch (*Betula nana*) is much smaller, often creeping, but occasionally erect in sheltered locations, where it grows knee-high. At ground level are two berry-bearing shrubs, the arctic blueberry (*Vaccinium uliginosum*) and crowberry (*Empetrum hermaphroditum*). Both are edible, but while most visiting walkers prefer the sweet blueberry, native Inuit prefer the slightly bitter crowberry.

Two other berry-bearing plants are often confused, the rock cranberry (*Vaccinium vitis-idaea*) and common bearberry (*Arctostaphylos uva-ursi*), both of which are red. An unmistakeable heath plant is the narrow-leaved Labrador tea (*Ledum palustre*), which has a sweet fragrance when crushed and makes a pleasant herbal drink. There are several species of cotton grass, including five Greenlandic species, of which the most common is the arctic cotton grass (*Eriophorum scheuchzeri*). Cotton grasses mark boggy ground, and when they are particularly dense they look like snow. Delicate horsetails (*Equisetum arvense*) are often salted throughout the heath and grow particularly thick on the disturbed ground beside roads. Grasses, sedges and rushes are abundant, while some species, such as

tall, tough-stalked lyme grass (*Elymus mollis*), favour dry, sandy, desert-like conditions.

Mosses and lichens are important components of the Arctic heaths. Some mosses are low-lying and need to be wet, while fir clubmosses (*Huperzia*) are tall, erect and tough, and can tolerate dry conditions. It is easy to mistake white arctic bell heather or moss heather (*Cassiope*) for clubmosses.

1 *Broad-leaved willow-herb, or niviarsiaq, meaning 'young woman', is Greenland's national flower*
2 *Crowberry is very common along the trail, and its berries, though slightly bitter, are perfectly edible*
3 *Among the fungi, boletus (or 'penny buns') provide an edible treat, seen here growing among dwarf birch*
4 *The red berries of rock cranberry are often confused with those of the common bearberry*

19

Among the lichens, 'reindeer moss' (*Cladonia*) is particularly favoured by reindeer. Fungi include edible varieties of boletus (*Leccinum*), also known as 'penny buns' or ceps, and puffballs, both useful for filling out the daily food rations. Ferns tend to grow in shaded, sheltered places, among boulders or in deep cracks in the bedrock.

Flowers are at their best in June and July, at the same time as mosquitoes, so few walkers will stop and admire them for long! Most notable up near the ice cap is the mountain avens (*Dryas integrifolia*). Watch for saxifrages (*Saxifraga*), daisy-like fleabanes (*Erigeron*) and gentians (*Gentiana/Gentianella*). Other flower 'families' include buttercup species (*Ranunculus*), cinquefoils (*Potentilla*) and plants such as stitchwort, pearlwort, sandwort and chickweed (*Nellike*). Arctic and common harebells (*Campanula*) last well into the summer, as does thrift (*Armeria scabra*). A particularly cheery plant is the broad-leafed willow-herb (*Chamaenerion latifolium*), Greenland's national flower, known as *niviarsiaq* (young woman). Its cousin fireweed (*Chamaenerion angustifolium*) might be noticed nearer to the coast, along with various dandelion species (*Taraxacum*), and possibly cluster-flowered lady's mantle (*Alchemilla glomerulans*) alongside streams. Common mare's tail (*Hippuris vulgaris*) is sometimes spotted growing in shallow pools.

A handy reference guide, in Danish and English, is *Grønlands Blomster – Flowers of Greenland*, published by Ahrent Flensborgs Forlag.

HISTORY

Over thousands of years, wave upon wave of human settlers broke along the coast of Greenland, and were in turn broken by the harshness of the terrain. The earliest settlers have been named after locations where similar cultures have been recorded, all in North America. The four main cultures are referred to as Independence, Saqqaq, Dorset and Thule. The Independence culture arrived around 2400BC and may have lasted for 800 years. The Saqqaq culture covered more territory, and existed around the same time as the Independence, but lasted for 1000 years. The Dorset culture may have sprung from either of the previous two cultures, arriving in two waves between 500BC and AD200. The Thule culture arrived around AD1200–1300, eventually spreading around the coast of Greenland. Their descendants remain to this day as the Inuit of Greenland. Inuit simply means 'people', and the name for Greenland, Kalaallit Nunaannut, means 'the land of the people'. The term 'Eskimo' is no longer used and can be considered offensive.

Norse involvement in Greenland could date from as early as AD930, when Gunnbjörn Ulfsson got blown off course, discovering land, but did not settle. In 978 the exiled Snæbjörn Galti settled at Bláserk Fjord, along with a bunch of desperadoes who promptly set about killing each other. Permanent settlement came with another exile in 982, when Eiríkr Rauði Þorvaldsson, or Erik the Red, sailed round southern Greenland. In 985, Erik convinced many Icelanders to join him in what he called 'Grænaland', choosing the name carefully so as to disguise its true nature. Out of 25 ships that set out, some were lost in storms and some turned back when they saw how inhospitable the place was, but 14 ship-loads made 'Greenland' their home.

Erik the Red's son, Leif Eriksson, visited Norway in the year 1000 and converted to Christianity. Later, losing his way home to Greenland, he apparently discovered North America. After settling briefly and calling the place Vinland, he returned to Greenland and set about converting the population to Christianity. The Norse settlers, despite all the hard work they put into their colony, were dependent on supplies from Norway, to which they became politically bound. However, Norway became caught up in European strife and warfare, losing the port of Bergen, and by the end of the 14th century was no longer in a position to supply such a far-flung outpost.

No-one knows what happened to the Norse settlers in Greenland. The final written record is of a wedding at Hvalsey in 1408, and soon afterwards the population simply vanished. With no historical account of their disappearance, all sorts of strange stories have been told, but for several

Looking across the lake (end of Day 6 and start of Day 7)

generations, the Inuit had the whole of Greenland to themselves.

In 1721 the Norwegian Lutheran Hans Egede headed a missionary expedition to Greenland. He wished to check if the Norse inhabitants had given up their faith or, worse, clung to pre-Reformation Catholicism long after Scandinavia had embraced Protestantism. Finding no trace of the old colony, Egede fixed his attention on the Inuit, established new colonies under Norwegian–Danish rule, and became known as the 'Apostle of Greenland'. His presence was seen as a threat by Dutch whalers, who caused him a lot of trouble.

Norway and Denmark were separated in 1814, and Denmark asserted full control over Greenland. However, the United States and Norway laid claim to parts of the country, and these claims were not settled until 1917 and 1933. During World War II, when Denmark was unable to supply Greenland, the United States was asked to administer affairs, and during the protectorate a number of air bases were established. American influence in Greenland remained strong afterwards, throughout the Cold War.

On 21 January 1968, near the Thule Air Base in northern Greenland, an American B-52 bomber crashed into the sea ice with four H-bombs on board. As the wreckage burnt, the ice melted and almost everything sank to the sea bed. A massive mid-winter clean-up was mounted, and, despite the secrecy surrounding the mission, it is understood that most of the components for three of the H-bombs were recovered. A vast amount of contaminated ice was removed to the United States for disposal. The fourth H-bomb remains lost.

The Cold War lasted until 1989, and, following its conclusion, US forces began dismantling their installations throughout Greenland. By the end of 1992 they had withdrawn, leaving only a token presence in the country.

From time to time, but notably throughout the 20th century, the majority Inuit population have called for greater autonomy. While Greenland automatically joined the European Union at the same time as Denmark in 1973, it became the first territory to withdraw from the Union, after a dispute over fishing rights in 1985. Increasingly vociferous calls for home rule continued. The nearby Northwest Territories of Canada became the new Inuit territory of Nunavut in 1999. Ten years later, Greenland was granted home rule on 21 June 2009.

In 2018 a strip of land stretching from the ice cap to the Davis Strait was designated as the 'Aasivissuit–Nipisat Inuit Hunting Ground between Ice and Sea' and inscribed on the World Heritage List. The Arctic Circle Trail enters this area after leaving the Canoe Centre on Day 4 and leaves it beyond Eqalugaarniarfik on Day 6. On the optional extension to the ice cap, another part of the area is passed through, between the ice cap and Aajuitsup Tasia, or Long Lake. The designated area contains the ruins of summer and winter camps and Inuit burial sites. The area is still used for reindeer and musk ox hunting.

CULTURE

The descendants of the Thule culture were the most successful occupants of Greenland. Unlike their predecessors, they had an array of tools and weapons to hunt and survive on land and sea. Their careful attention to making sealskin clothing ensured that they remained warm and dry in harsh conditions, while the construction of snow and ice dwellings was an ingenious achievement.

Traditional songs and stories were passed on orally through Inuit culture, but words were not to be bandied around lightly. Words had the power to charm or to harm, and as a result were used sparingly. Maybe it was a reflection of the huge, empty, silent landscapes around them, but the Inuit traditionally regarded silence to be as important as sound. Their animist reverence for the world around them ensured that no animal was killed unless it was for food, and that no waste remained. Bones were carved into tools, and pelts made into clothing. What little that remained of a kill would be fed to the dogs on which the Inuit relied for rapid transport across the frozen wastes.

From the 18th century Danish colonial names began to appear on

Greenlandic Inuit have had to adapt quickly from nomadic hunter-gatherers to a Western lifestyle

the map of Greenland, frequently recalling kings, queens and princes. Even the Prince of Wales got his name on one bleak area! Søndre Strømfjord separated Kong Frederik IX Land from Dronning Ingrid Land, while nearby coastal settlements were named Godthåb and Holsteinsborg. With the increasing reassertion of Inuit culture, these colonial names have reverted to Inuit forms. However, maps of Greenland are full of blank spaces, and the few Inuit names that appear often translate into mundane things. Tasersuaq simply means 'big lake'. Names, to the Inuit, are sacred and bear souls of their own, which flicker and dance among the northern lights until called to earth. The assumption must be made that the over-use of names might cause those lights to go out!

One man who made an invaluable record of traditional Inuit culture was Knud Rasmussen, born in Greenland in 1879, the son of a Lutheran minister. He studied in Denmark, worked as a journalist, and in 1902 joined an expedition in Greenland run by Mylius Erichsen. For the first time in his life, Rasmussen encountered the Inuit living in the most remote parts of the country. He established the Thule station, from where he launched seven expeditions. His fifth expedition ran from 1921 to 1924, using dog-sleds to explore all the way across northern Canada to Siberia. This was the longest journey of its kind through the polar region, establishing contact with the most remote Inuit settlements, while

studying the topography and archaeology along the way.

Shortly after completing his seventh expedition in 1933 Rasmussen died in Copenhagen, having amassed the most important collection of polar artefacts in the world, recording Inuit culture and publishing a series of books on the subject. One wonders if he might have preferred to die in Greenland. In the past, traditional Inuit burial places were marked by simple cairns, situated in locations enjoying exceptional views over water.

Traditional arts and crafts are enjoying something of a revival in Greenland. The carved bones known as *tupilaq* were originally simple bones laden with magic spells to defeat an enemy. Now they are intricately carved and imaginatively designed as innocuous giftware. The sealskin trade was almost wiped out due to adverse publicity in recent decades, which seems unfair, as Greenlanders never engaged in brutal practices. CITES certificates can be provided for legitimately produced items, should you have any concerns about purchasing goods and getting them home through customs.

Harvesting the sea provides employment for many Greenlanders, and it is surprising how many packs of Greenland prawns make their way onto the shelves of British supermarkets. Many Greenlanders have a very modern outlook, and, despite the population numbering a mere 57,000 souls, produce fashion goods, arts and crafts, as well as marketing their own brand of popular music and culture.

TRAVELLING TO GREENLAND

Greenland, whether you are coming from Europe or the US, is best reached from Copenhagen in Denmark. Direct flights operate from Copenhagen to Kangerlussuaq, the international airport for the whole of Greenland. Air Greenland, www.airgreenland.com, uses an Airbus 330-200, usually flying daily. Anyone wishing to walk the Arctic Circle trail in reverse can fly onwards from Kangerlussuaq to Sisimiut in a matter of minutes on a Dash-8-200, usually twice daily, but check for exact schedules.

There are also flights from Iceland to Greenland, but these are awkward for anyone walking the Arctic Circle Trail, as onward flights are needed to reach Kangerlussuaq. Charter flights to Greenland are sometimes available.

If travel to Greenland cannot be accomplished in a day then take the opportunity to stay overnight – or maybe longer – in Copenhagen, and make a city break out of it.

Note that there are plans to construct new airports in Greenland, with long runways. This could result in the downgrading of Kangerlussuaq, which in turn could make it more difficult and expensive to access the Arctic Circle Trail.

Travel to Copenhagen
By air
Every country in Europe has direct flights to Copenhagen. British cities with direct flights include London, Birmingham, Manchester, Newcastle, Glasgow, Edinburgh and Aberdeen. Most are operated by Scandinavian

Signpost at the airport at Kangerlussuaq. Welcome to the Arctic Circle. Next stop the North Pole!

Airlines (SAS), www.flysas.com, but others include Norwegian, www.norwegian.com; British Airways, www.britishairways.com; and EasyJet, www.easyjet.com. SAS also has direct flights to Copenhagen from Chicago, New York (Newark) and Washington DC.

By train
Copenhagen can be reached by train from Britain via France, Belgium and Germany. The trip from London to Copenhagen can be accomplished in less than 24 hours. Check various options with 'The Man in Seat 61', www.seat61.com.

By coach
The journey from London to Copenhagen can be completed using Eurolines coaches, www.eurolines.com. Leave London in the afternoon, change late at night in Brussels, and reach Copenhagen the following afternoon. The journey time is less than 24 hours.

Copenhagen
If staying overnight in Copenhagen, the city has abundant accommodation and an excellent public transport system, www.copenhagen.com.

Travel around Greenland
There are no long roads connecting settlements in Greenland. Travel between settlements is mainly by air, although ferries and cruise ships also provide links around the coast. Anyone planning to explore

A dog sled at Old Camp (Day 1)

Greenland beyond the Arctic Circle Trail is warned that it can become very expensive, very quickly, because of escalating travel costs.

WHEN TO GO

The Arctic Circle Trail is essentially a summer trek, but bear in mind that summer at this latitude is very brief. Anyone attempting the trail in May would probably need snowshoes, while rivers and lakes may well be frozen. The thaw starts early in June, when river crossings are at their deepest, coldest and most dangerous, although here is continual daylight. The celebrated Midnight

Sun cannot be seen from the trail, since there are mountains in the way. Taking a midsummer boat trip from Sisimiut allows the Midnight Sun to be observed.

From mid-June mosquitoes and biting flies can be most irritating, and as the days get warmer through July they assume plague proportions. From mid-August, the first few frosty nights will get rid of almost all of them, and this can be the best time to walk the trail. By mid-September, the days shorten dramatically, and winter could make itself felt at any time. As the nights lengthen, however, there are opportunities to see the northern lights. From October to May, assume that the Arctic Circle Trail is covered in snow.

Two winter events deserve a mention, as they are held at either end of the Arctic Circle Trail. The Polar Circle Marathon, www. polar-circle-marathon.com, takes place in October between the ice cap and Kangerlussuaq, lasting only for a day. The Arctic Circle Race, www.acr.gl, takes place in March on parts of the trail near Sisimiut, lasting two or three days. Local people travel along the Arctic Circle Trail in dog-sleds and snowmobiles during the winter, covering the route at speed. They vary the route by tearing across frozen lakes, instead of following narrow paths alongside. The record for the snowmobile trip between Kangerlussuaq and Sisimiut is a little over 1½ hours!

ACCOMMODATION

Accommodation is available in Kangerlussuaq and Sisimiut, at either end of the trail, with a variety of services available at a range of prices. Options range from a basic campsite and comfortable hostels to expensive hotels. The only accommodation provided along the trail is in the form of basic, unstaffed trail huts, while camping is possible in many places. See the descriptions of Kangerlussuaq and Sisimiut to find details of accommodation options. Individual descriptions of each of the huts along the trail are given at the end of each daily stage.

Budget accommodation is available at the Kangerlussuaq Vandrehjem

Wild camping is free and virtually unrestricted along the whole of the Arctic Circle Trail (Day 8)

The huts along the Arctic Circle Trail vary in size, sleeping anything from six to 22 people in varying degrees of comfort. Stories have been told of huts that sleep six being occupied by 20 or more people! While some have bunk beds with mattresses, others have only a wooden sleeping platform, and none of them have bedding. They are unstaffed and offer no services, so you need to carry your own mattress, sleeping bag, food, stove and fuel. The huts can't be booked in advance, but on the other hand the only limit on occupancy is how tolerant people are to overcrowding. While most trekkers will budge

28

up and make room for you, some groups have been reported to be very rude and refused entry to others. A tent is good insurance against an overcrowded hut!

TOILETS

Only a few of the huts contain toilets, and these are very basic 'bag-in-a-bin' affairs. If you use these toilets, then you must assume responsibility for emptying them when they are one-third full. Do this by releasing the top of the plastic bag, folding it and clipping it, then carry the bag outside and leave it in one of the lockers provided. Place a new bag in the bin. If you refuse to empty these toilets then you have no right to use them. Once the bag is more than half full it becomes difficult to deal with, and any more than that makes the task increasingly unpleasant and difficult. No-one wants to sleep in a hut containing a bin overflowing with human waste.

Far too many trekkers treat the trail as an open toilet. The areas around the huts can be particularly bad, and many of the level areas that should be idyllic campsites are liberally strewn with faeces. When there are no toilets available, the only way to 'go' is to do it in a manner that leaves absolutely no trace whatsoever. Just walk off the trail and away from water, dig a hole with the heel of your boot or use a trekking pole, and afterwards cover it up.

For a fuller explanation, and for the sheer joy of reading an excellent book on the subject, get a copy of *How to Shit in the Woods*, by Kathleen Meyer, published by Ten Speed Press. If you can't do it discreetly, without leaving a trace, then please don't plan a trek along the Arctic Circle Trail, and instead choose another trail with the sort of facilities that make you feel comfortable.

HEALTH AND SAFETY

Trekkers must be completely self-sufficient on the Arctic Circle Trail, and must carry everything they need to deal with any eventuality that might arise. Minor ailments can be treated at a nursing station at the airport at Kangerlussuaq, tel 86 88 12. Anything major is probably best dealt with at the hospital at Sisimiut, tel 86 42 11. If you need regular medication, take an ample supply. If you need any assistance along the trail, and especially in the remote middle stages, then it could take time for anyone to reach you.

In case of injury or illness, there are really only three ways to deal with a situation. One is to sort things out for yourself, which is probably the best thing to do if problems are minor. Another is to seek assistance from anyone else that might be on the trail, but bear in mind that even if they are willing to assist, it is going to cause them inconvenience. Finally, in extreme cases, it might be necessary to call for a rescue. Bear in mind that in doing so you might be putting the lives of the rescuers at risk. The first point of contact is the police. Ring Sisimiut, tel 70 13 22, or 70 14 48 in the evenings; or Kangerlussuaq, tel 70 13 24 or 70 14 48 in the evenings.

Mobile phones don't work on the trail, and while some trekkers carry satellite phones, making a call doesn't guarantee an instant response. A helicopter rescue was mounted for a heart attack victim in 2018, but didn't reach the casualty for six hours. In a couple of instances injured trekkers have pretty much rescued themselves when no-one else was available to help. Tread carefully and don't take unnecessary risks.

FOOD, DRINK AND FUEL

Greenland is self-sufficient in sea-food, reindeer and musk oxen, along with mushrooms and wild berries in the summer, but most other foodstuffs are imported and are quite expensive. Costs can be kept to a minimum by bringing as much 'trekking' food as possible into the country, though you will have to purchase stove fuel on arrival. It would be a great pity to miss sampling some of the local fare, but be prepared to pay a high price for such treats. Interestingly, there are hardly any poisonous plants in Greenland, so, with a little care, walkers can experiment with almost anything that grows. Some try their hand at fishing, with mixed results. Occasionally, walkers meet local hunters and are often pleasantly surprised to be invited to impromptu cook-outs in the wilds. Never say no to such invitations!

Stove fuel is available at either end of the trail, including a variety of pierceable and resealable gas canisters, and a number of flammable liquids. The latter are bottled by a company called Borup, www.borup.info, and you should check in advance which ones will work with your stove, otherwise it becomes a matter of guesswork on the supermarket shelves. Methylated spirit is known as *husholdnings sprit*. Paraffin or kerosene is *lampeolie*. Petroleum, white gas or naphtha is *benzin*. Wood for camp-fires is exceedingly scarce and twiggy. Following extensive fires on the trail in 2016, 2017 and 2019, it is probably best to avoid starting any kind of fire, and to take extreme care using stoves

A skilful conversion of a standard trekking pole into a fishing rod, which actually caught an arctic char!

outdoors. The problem with fires on the tundra is that the vegetation takes decades to recover, and the underlying peat can burn underground for several weeks. Fire extinguishers, beaters and portable water containers with hoses have been placed at huts along the route. In case of fire, it is hoped that trekkers will take immediate action, as it is impossible for the fire departments in Kangerlussuaq or Sisimiut to attend such fires.

Water is fresh and abundant along the Arctic Circle Trail, and you must ensure that it remains in that state. If you foul the water, it could lead to someone dying. Generally, running water is scarce, but cups, pans and bottles of water can generally be scooped up from lakes and consumed without the need for treatment. The slightly brackish lakes at Tarajornitsut are an exception, but even consuming this water is unlikely to be a problem.

LANGUAGE

Greenlandic is the native language of the country, spoken by 50,000 of its inhabitants, along with 7000 Greenlanders living in Denmark. There are four main dialects – north, east, west and Thule. West Greenlandic, or Kalaallisut, is spoken at either end of the Arctic Circle Trail. There are few opportunities for visitors to learn Greenlandic, but it is courteous to be able to speak at least a few words. The spoken word is very soft and can be difficult to pronounce. The written word is quite complicated, to the extent that a whole sentence can become a single word containing lots of double letters and a surfeit of qs.

Danish, the colonial language, is of course widely spoken and is taught alongside Greenlandic in schools, so it can be helpful to know some basic words and phrases. As some old Norse/Danish elements have long been incorporated into the English language, some words are easily understood. Many people working regularly with tourists speak English, and despite the increasing number of nationalities seen along the Arctic Circle Trail, English is commonly spoken throughout. See Appendix B for translations between English, Danish and Greenlandic.

MONEY

Greenland could be one of the most expensive places you are ever likely to visit, but the Arctic Circle Trail can be completed on a very low budget. There is no escaping the cost of flights to and from Greenland, and for most travellers there are also the costs of flights to and from Copenhagen. Most walkers will incur the additional cost of a one-way flight from the end of the trail at Sisimiut to the international airport at Kangerlussuaq. The total for all these flights, maybe five in all, might come to around £1000.

The Danish krone is used throughout Greenland, and it is best

31

Some walkers head for a bar at the end of the trail, but the author prefers the café at the bakery

to take a good supply in the form of cash. Credit cards are accepted by many businesses, but sometimes the only card acceptable is Dankort. There is no bank in Kangerlussuaq, but there is an ATM at the airport, so cash can be obtained for immediate purchases at the start of the Arctic Circle Trail. Cash is quite useless on the trail itself, unless you are thinking of buying things from other trekkers! Money supplies can be replenished at a bank or ATM once Sisimiut is reached at the end of the trail.

Trying to work out a budget for the trip involves all kinds of variables, but some things are certain. Costs within Greenland for food, accommodation and transport are often excessive, but walkers on the Arctic Circle Trail can, with careful planning, manage on a shoestring. Indeed, canny walkers may be able to avoid paying for anything beyond the flights to and from the country, providing that they take all their food with them and spend all their nights camping.

The best way to avoid the cost of the flight at the end of the trail from Sisimiut to Kangerlussuaq is to walk back – seriously! Even buying expensive food in Sisimiut will be cheaper than the cost of a flight, and you can enjoy the whole of the Arctic Circle Trail for a second time. The author has done this and thoroughly enjoyed it.

All walkers on the trail have to carry their own food. It is much cheaper to source specialist 'trekking' food at home than in Greenland, and the range of menus available will be much wider at home.

Nearly all walkers on the trail carry a tent, and there is no charge for wild camping. Huts along the trail are available free of charge, but as they cannot be booked in advance, and are unstaffed, it's a case of 'first come, first served'.

So, the whole of the Arctic Circle Trail can be walked twice, costing nothing more than the price of food bought in your home country. However, it would be a pity not to sample local foodstuffs, so be sure to pack some Danish krone and a credit card, and support the Greenlandic economy in some way.

COMMUNICATIONS

The country code for Greenland is +299, if phoning from outside the country. There are no area codes so just dial the telephone number you require. Tele-Post Centres (post offices) and telephones are located at either end of the Arctic Circle Trail, in Kangerlussuaq and Sisimiut. Enquire locally about wi-fi hotspots, and note that most hotels and hostels have systems for the use of residents, but expect to pay a high price. Mobile phone reception is good in Kangerlussuaq and Sisimiut, but completely absent for the length of the Arctic Circle Trail. Note that Greenland is probably not covered by 'roaming' agreements with your provider, and calls might cost as much as £1 or £2 per minute. If a telephone is deemed essential on the trail, there is no option but to hire or invest in an expensive satellite model, but please ensure that you are familiar with its operation. If travelling in a group, there are devices that act as a hub, allowing a small number of mobile phones to connect simultaneously with a satellite. The bottom line with 'keeping in touch' is that it's a very expensive business in Greenland!

TREKKING IN GREENLAND

The green edges of Greenland, at least in the summer months, are ideal for walking. A series of 'Hiking Maps' at a scale of 1:100,000 (see 'Maps' below) suggest a number of trails, but these

A dirt road approaches the Sugar Loaf, which could be climbed using a path on the far side

Walking beside a lake towards the end of Day 8

are often only 'suggestions', and there may not actually be a trodden route on the ground. Sometimes, the nature of the terrain is so difficult as to be impassable, but most of the time the low-lying Arctic scrub is very forgiving and allows routes to be followed in all directions. An ability to 'read' the terrain is as important as the ability to read a map.

The Arctic Circle Trail is unusual in that it is almost entirely along a trodden path from start to finish, equipped with basic huts at regular intervals and 'wild' tent pitches wherever you can find a suitable space on the ground. The trail is only rarely signposted, but at regular intervals its course is indicated by cairns supplemented by a red semi-circular paint mark. These often

fade to orange or pink, or wash away completely, but they are refreshed from time to time. The semi-circle is derived from the design in the centre of the Greenlandic national flag. Some cairns are attractively adorned with reindeer antlers and so are very distinctive.

The Arctic Circle Trail measures 165km (103 miles) between Kangerlussuaq and Sisimiut, and most walkers cover the distance in anything from a week to 10 days. Anyone taking advantage of all the huts will spend nine days on the trail. The distance can be extended to run all the way from the ice cap (see Optional Extension) to Sisimiut, measuring a total of 202km (125½ miles). The trail is not in itself difficult, but it can seem so in bad

Mountains and Lakes feature throughout Day 6

weather or while burdened with a heavy load. It is also very remote, so it is not recommended for a first-time backpacker, but is eminently suitable for anyone who has previous experience of being self-sufficient for several days on a trail. Few trekkers experience any route-finding difficulties, but maps and the ability to use them should be considered essential. The trail mostly follows a narrow, trodden path, but this can be vague in places. Cairns have been built at intervals, painted with red semi-circles. There are only a handful of signposts, and most of these are located near the huts.

In wet weather, and particularly at the height of the thaw, those parts of the trail crossing boggy ground will be completely saturated. Some bogs never dry out, while others become completely desiccated if they are subjected to several days of strong, dry easterly winds. Generally, the weather will be better in late summer than in early summer, and the likelihood is that the ground underfoot will be drier later, rather than earlier. It is impossible to predict the weather, which is changeable, and even if you obtain a forecast at the start of a walk along the trail, it won't be valid for more than half of the trek.

One stretch of the Arctic Circle Trail doesn't have to be walked, as the long lake of Amitsorsuaq can be covered by paddling a canoe. Over the years, the number of canoes decreased as they were lost, sunk or damaged beyond repair. A new fleet of canoes was in place for the 2022

35

season, but not everyone will treat these with the respect they require. Some will be abandoned, then become lost or sunk, while the paddles and lifejackets will inevitably go missing due to carelessness. You use these canoes at your own risk, and you must use them responsibly, and never abandon or damage them.

RIVER CROSSINGS

There are a handful of river crossings on the Arctic Circle Trail when water levels are high. You should only attempt these if you feel you have the skills and knowledge to do so. Walkers with experience of fording rivers will know what is required, while others should proceed with caution, following the advice below and bearing in mind that every river and every ford is different. On the Arctic Circle Trail, the greatest amount of water flows in June, as snow and ice melt early in the summer. Towards the end of summer, during September, the water flow is much less and rivers are lower, but an unusual spell of wet weather will cause a sudden increase.

Before stepping into a river, walk up and downstream to select a suitable ford. Narrow stretches are invariably deepest, and may feature the strongest currents. Broad stretches are usually shallowest, but beware of broad bends, as the water may be shallow on one side and deep on the other, or feature an undercut riverbank that prevents exit. If a river is

deep and swift, then don't cross, but look elsewhere. If a river is broad and shallow, it may be possible to hop dry-shod from boulder to boulder, but only do this is you are sure-footed. Avoid wet and greasy boulders which may result in an awkward fall.

Crossing a river barefoot is not recommended. Sharp or uneven stones can injure feet, and progress is likely to be slow, with walkers standing too long in cold water. Remove socks to keep them dry, then either put walking boots or shoes back on, or change them for something else. 'Crocs', for example, are very light and were designed for river crossings. Ensure that your pack hip-belt and chest strap are unfastened. In the event of falling in deep water, discard your pack. Trekking poles are immensely useful for balance and for probing the river bed before each step. Proceed cautiously with short steps. With two feet and two poles, ensure that there are always three points of contact with the riverbed. If travelling without poles, two or more people can cross effectively by holding onto each other.

Rivers less than knee-deep are unlikely to pose problems. Rivers running higher, or running swiftly, must be approached with utmost care. There comes a point, which varies from person to person, where the force of water cannot be resisted. Some say you should angle your crossing to walk slightly against the current, while others say you should angle your crossing to walk with the current. In practice, walkers might need to go against and with the current. Cautious walkers will retreat if things aren't going their way, but if suddenly swept away, the important thing is to get rid of your pack, then scramble or swim to one of the banks as quickly as possible. Save your life before trying to salvage your gear, and bear in mind that the more things you pack in waterproof liners, the more things will survive total immersion. Despite their apparent weight and bulk, most packs will float!

Deep and fast-flowing rivers have hidden dangers and should only be crossed by those with experience. For those walking as part of a group, if you know that there are difficult crossings ahead, then a rope should be carried, and members can assist each other across. If walking solo, proceed with extreme caution. (Solo river crossings are more hazardous but may be necessary.) The most radical river crossing would involve a solo walker, with no safety rope, getting into deep, cold, fast-flowing water, having lashed their pack to an inflatable mattress to form a flotation device. Maintaining a line across a river in these conditions would be extremely difficult, but it has been done on the Arctic Circle Trail!

River crossings at either end of the Arctic Circle Trail are unlikely to be a problem. The most awkward is in the middle, at Itinneq (Ole's Lakseelv). If conditions are such that the river is impassable, the river can be crossed using a footbridge, but bear in mind

that a pathless bog must be traversed to reach it. Those who are simply trying to avoid wet feet generally agree that the detour to the bridge isn't worth the effort, and their feet usually get wet anyway. Those who are trying to preserve their lives, however, will be grateful for the bridge no matter how much effort is needed to reach it.

WHAT TO TAKE

Walkers heading into the wilds of Greenland need to be completely self-sufficient in terms of clothing and shelter from the elements, with

Be warned that mosquito nets might be required in high summer!

enough food for the duration of their trek, possibly supplemented by basic hunter-gatherer skills. Water is abundant and normally does not need to be purified or carried any great distance. However, it is useful to have water containers, simply to avoid traipsing back and forth between an overnight camp and water supply.

On the Arctic Circle Trail, carry enough food to last one or two more days than you intend to spend on the trek. If a day off is taken, or if bad weather forces any delay, at least you will have enough to eat. Similarly with fuel, take a little more than you think you will need. Sometimes, trekkers who are overburdened will off-load fuel and foodstuffs at one of the huts, which is then available for anyone who needs extra supplies. Dehydrated 'trekking' food will appeal because of its low weight and bulk, but you should satisfy yourself that this will meet your energy needs. For a psychological boost, don't forget to pack a few treats, whether that be chocolate, dried fruit or your favourite tipple.

Naturally, anyone walking north of the Arctic Circle will be concerned about cold weather, but many trekkers over-dress on this trail, or at least carry too many clothes. In this respect, bear in mind that Arctic summers are often remarkably warm and pleasantly fresh. Walkers sometimes trek the route in shorts and tee-shirts, and require plenty of sunscreen.

However, there may be chilly periods, possibly rain, wind and even

snow, so be sure to pack warm and waterproof clothing. The usual three-layer approach should work fine – thermal base layer, warmer mid-layer, and a waterproof outer layer. As a general rule, expect an Arctic summer to be roughly equivalent to good British spring or autumn weather. While the sun may not rise high, nor feel particularly warm at times, it hangs in the sky for much longer.

The wind normally blows from the east or west. When it blows from the west, coming from the sea, expect thick cloud, perhaps mist and rain, and a general lowering of the temperature. It can snow in the summer, but this is very rare and it will be very short-lived on the ground. When the wind blows from the east, it may be chilly, as it comes from the ice cap, but it will generally be clear and sunny too, and any sheltered spot is a sun-trap. The east wind is often very dry, so if you wash any clothes, hang them in a sunny, windy spot and they will dry remarkably quickly. Even wet boots can be completely dried in a few hours.

Footwear is a personal choice. Some parts of the trail are wet and boggy, but most parts are firm and dry. When it rains, brushing past willow and birch scrub could cause wet feet. The only sure protection would be to wear wellingtons, but these would be cumbersome, requiring long socks to avoid chaffing, while taking every opportunity to vent them to avoid a build-up of condensation.

Some people wear heavy, unyielding boots, which seems quite unnecessary. One interesting compromise is be to wear lightweight boots, with little or no chance of keeping water out, coupled with 'Sealskinz' socks, which are waterproof and breathable. Most of the time, feet will stay dry, even if the outside of the socks and the boots are sodden, but take care not to scuff or puncture the socks. Gaiters will prevent some water ingress and prevent irritating sand, grit, leaves and twigs from entering footwear. In fine weather socks and footwear can be dried easily in the evenings. An Inuit walker on the Arctic Circle Trail, a man who once walked the trail in only three days, proudly revealed his own solution for keeping his socks dry – wearing plastic bags over them!

As discussed in more detail in the previous section, for the handful of river crossings along the trail, trekking poles are advisable. You could also pack something like a pair of lightweight 'Crocs', which were designed for fording rivers, and which also prove excellent for wandering around in the evening, when boots are drying.

Sometimes, when walkers take shelter in one of the huts and its turns chilly, they wonder whether they can get the paraffin-fuelled 'Refleks' heaters to work. Please, only attempt to light one of these heaters if you are absolutely sure of what you are doing. They get so hot that the metal turns red. Used wrongly, or with the wrong fuel, they can burn down a hut or cause carbon monoxide poisoning or even an explosion. The heaters are fuelled with paraffin (Danish – *lampeolie*), and full instructions for safe use can be obtained from the Refleks website, www.refleks-olieovne.dk.

Although you need to be completely self-sufficient on the Arctic Circle Trail, as far as possible try to pack lightweight, low-bulk kit. Many people trek with huge and bulky packs, up to a capacity of 80 litres, weighing as much as 35 kilos. The author manages fine with half that weight and capacity, without sacrificing anything in terms of food or comfort. Don't make life difficult for yourself by carrying a pack that is far too heavy and cumbersome.

WAYMARKING AND ACCESS

The Arctic Circle Trail was first marked in the 1990s by widely spaced cairns daubed with a semi-circle of red paint. In the early years, there were barely any trodden paths, and the first walkers on the trail had to pick their way through the low Arctic scrub to get from one cairn to another. Most of the time they chose good lines, which became narrow paths. Occasionally, they didn't choose a good line, ploughing through bogs that might have been best avoided. Many walkers have literally 'voted with their feet', short-cutting corners and leaving some paint-marked cairns marooned in areas without the slightest trace of a path. A few signposts have been

Map, compass, GPS and the ability to use them are essential on the trail (Day 4)

This leaves today's walkers with a few little quandaries. Should they follow the 'true' Arctic Circle Trail, as marked by the cairns? Or should they walk in the footsteps of others? A third possibility is to stick rigidly to the trail marked on maps, which occasionally varies from both the cairned and trodden route. In the end, walkers must decide for themselves how they will deal with fine details on an hour-by-hour basis. The only place where a significant choice of routes occurs is on Day 5 at the crossing of Itinneq (or Ole's Lakseelv). This is the widest and deepest river that needs to be forded, and occasionally it is best avoided, in which case a pathless variant route leads to a footbridge.

installed in recent years, but most of these are near the huts, where they aren't really needed.

Magnetic Variation along the Trail 2014–2023					
	longitude	*latitude*	*2014*	*2023*	*changin*
Kangerlussuaq	50° 41' W	67° 34' N	30° 18' W	26° 32' W	0° 26'
Eqalugaarniarfik	52° 20' W	67° 00' N	30° 54' W	27° 00' W	0° 26'
Sisimiut	53° 40' W	66° 56' N	31° 20' W	27° 19' W	0° 26'

Source: US National Geophysical Data Center of the National Oceanic and Atmospheric Administ (NOAA)

Bear in mind that the path under-foot becomes better trodden every year as more people walk it. As a result, route-finding should become easier over time, with one continuous trodden path evolving.

MAPS

Three 'Hiking Maps' at a scale of 1:100,000 cover the Arctic Circle Trail, published by Greenland Tourism, with cartography by the Scottish company Harvey Map Services. The contour interval is 25m (82ft), which is enough to hide several significant ups and downs. The maps are waterproof, and the reverse is printed with additional useful information. Despite the limitations of scale the maps are excellent, and extracts are used throughout this guide; the route has been highlighted and extra route information added to correspond with the trail description in this guide.

Note the huge magnetic declination in this region before attempting to navigate with a map and compass. Read and understand the notes printed on the maps. Note the provision of blue grid lines indicating the direction of the magnetic north pole. Take sample bearings as early as possible to ensure you understand the system and are confident with its operation – before you find yourself in mist!

Winding creeks fill with water at high tide at the head of the fjord at Maligiaq, near the Eqalugaarniarfik Hut (Day 6)

Purchase the required map sheets, 'Kangerlussuaq', 'Pingu' and 'Sisimiut', in advance of travel, though they are on sale in Kangerlussuaq and Sisimiut. The maps are available from Harvey Map Services, 12–22 Main Street, Doune, FK16 6BJ, tel 01786 841202, www.harveymaps. co.uk; Stanfords, 7 Mercer Walk, Covent Garden, London, WC2H 9FA, tel 020 7836 1321, www.stanfords. co.uk; The Map Shop, 15 High Street, Upton upon Severn, Worcestershire, WR8 0HJ, tel 01684 593146, www. themapshop.co.uk; and Cordee www. cordee.co.uk.

The Hiking Maps are also available in digital form for use on an electronic device. First download the 'Avenza Maps' app, then go to the 'Store' and find Greenland on the map. The three maps between Kangerlussuaq and Sisimiut can be downloaded for a payment, roughly half the price of the printed maps. Using the app, it is possible to enlarge the mapping considerably on the screen, for easier viewing. GPX tracks for each stage of the trail can be downloaded from the Cicerone website.

Several 'Saga Maps' are available, with a selection of them covering the whole of Greenland at various scales, www.sagamaps.com. A series of 18 maps at a scale of 1:250,000 cover almost the whole western side of the country between the ice cap and the sea. Four more cover small parts of East Greenland. Sheet number 8,

'Sisimiut Kangerlussuaq', covers the area traversed by the Arctic Circle Trail. While it is a useful map in terms of offering an overview of the landscape on a single sheet, the map is not recommended for trekking, and the course of the Arctic Circle Trail is not shown.

Arctic Sun Maps produce a 'Kangerlussuaq-Sisimiut' sheet at a scale of 1:250,000, showing the Arctic Circle Trail. There is also a 'Kangerlussuaq' map at a scale of 1:50,000. See www.arcticsunmaps. weebly.com or look out for them once in Greenland.

While Google Street View claims to cover the Arctic Circle Trail, this isn't strictly true. The route displayed is the one used by snowmobiles travelling in winter between Kangerlussuaq and Sisimiut. Snowmobiles rarely follow the trodden path, and naturally they scoot across frozen lakes instead of following rugged shoreline paths. By all means check Street View, but it doesn't look anything like the Arctic Circle Trail in summer.

EMERGENCIES

It used to be common for walkers to register their departure on the Arctic Circle Trail with the Politi (police) in Kangerlussuaq. Details were then emailed to the police in Sisimiut. However, many trekkers failed to announce their safe arrival and increasing numbers of trekkers made the system unworkable. Please leave a note of your intended trek dates with a reliable contact, who should take full responsibility for alerting the police should they fail to hear from you within a reasonable time after your intended finish. If you don't get in touch with your contact, then they will have to decide whether you need assistance. For the police in Sisimiut, tel 70 13 22, or 70 14 48 in the evenings; or for the police in Kangerlussuaq, tel 70 13 24 or 70 14 48 in the evenings.

For many years, no-one needed to be rescued from the Arctic Circle Trail, but with its increasing popularity, there have been a few instances where rescues have been mounted. Please note that the population is sparse and there simply aren't enough people available to take part in a rescue at short notice. If you are 'walking wounded' then it might be best to keep walking. In case of more serious need it might still be possible for your companions or other trekkers to assist. In case of immediate assistance being required, a satellite phone will be required to make contact with the police, then the police will decide what sort of assistance might be provided. Bear in mind that a helicopter evacuation could take hours to organise and someone has to pay the bill. Many insurance policies would class a walk along the Arctic Circle Trail as a hazardous pursuit, so before relying on an insurance company to pay the bill, be sure that you have adequate cover.

If a rescue takes several hours, the casualty needs to be kept warm, sheltered and comfortable. Anyone staying with them will be delayed

The trail is sparsely signposted so mapreading skills are useful

Don't carry too much as it becomes slow and exhausting

and could lose a day's trekking, in which case they will need to be carrying enough food to enable them to complete the trek. Maybe they could relieve the casualty of their food, if they no longer need it!

ALL CHANGE ON THE TRAIL

For many years there were plans to construct a road linking Kangerlussuaq and Sisimiut. When the Arctic Circle Trail was walked by the author in 2018, in order to create a new edition of this guidebook for 2019, these plans were still being discussed. However, there was a sudden push for funding and the road was rapidly constructed through the summers of 2020 and 2021.

Bearing in mind that the author hasn't had an opportunity to visit the area since the road was constructed, the following notes explain what trekkers need to be aware of, until such time as a new edition of this guidebook becomes available.

The road doesn't affect the entire Arctic Circle Trail, and it isn't suitable for all types of vehicle. Trekkers starting in Kangerlussuaq always had to walk along a road until they passed Kelly Ville.

The new dirt road has been designed for ATV (quad bike) use. It runs onto the tundra to pass the lake of Hundesø. Trekkers should leave the road in order to follow the Arctic Circle Trail past the lake of Limnæso and stay on the cairn-marked trodden path across the tundra towards the lake of Qarlissuit.

The Arctic Circle Trail continues exactly as described in the guidebook, without any intersection with the ATV road from Day 2 to Day 5, reaching the hut at Eqalugaarniarfik. However, anyone attempting to follow the original trail beyond the hut will soon run into the ATV road again at Iluliumanersuup Portornga. The trail and dirt road more or less follow the same course throughout the rest of Day 6 until arriving in Sisimiut on Day 9. The road is visually intrusive, but is unlikely to be busy in the immediate future. In the more distant future there is a plan to construct a road for cars and tour buses.

Some trekkers might follow the road in the hope of easier progress, while others might prefer to keep away from it for as long as possible. A new stretch of the Arctic Circle Trail is now available, leaving the hut at Eqalugaarniarfik to head towards the inlet of Maligiaq. The new trail is marked with cairns and should become a trodden path in places, but the terrain is quite rugged, along with a series of ascents and descents. There are camping spaces at intervals and there is a plan to build one or two huts. The new trail is marked on the latest Compukort Pingu map.

Trekkers who follow the new trail pass within sight of a small village called Sarfannguit, where there is a useful shop. However, the village is located on an island, so it is necessary to attract the attention of a boatman in order to visit. It is hoped that a flag or signal might be installed to help with this crossing.

If not visiting Sarfannguit, the trail climbs high through rugged terrain and later descends to an inlet at Utoqqaat. After climbing through a gap in the mountains, the new trail links with the original course of the Arctic Circle Trail near the end of Day 8 at Kangerluarsuk Tulleq, re-joining the course of the dirt road.

There is little opportunity for trekkers to avoid the dirt road on Day 9 to finish in Sisimiut. The provision of a road linking Kangerlussuaq and Sisimiut is bound to attract the attention of cyclists, who might wonder if they can bike-pack the route. By all accounts the road surface is quite rough, but experienced dirt road cyclists could cope. It is likely that some trekkers might prefer to walk along the dirt road in the hope that it will offer them easier navigation, but there are currently no huts offering shelter except for those already existing at Hundesø and Kangerluarsuk Tulleq.

Kangerlussuaq airport is likely to be downgraded in the future

USING THIS GUIDE

The Arctic Circle Trail is described from east to west, from Kangerlussuaq to Sisimiut (see Appendix A for a route summary). An extension at the beginning of the route is possible (Optional Extension), starting from the ice cap or Russells Glacier. There is no problem walking the entire route in the opposite direction, apart from having to reverse all the route directions. The maps and waymarks work just as well one way as they do the other.

The guidebook has sections on Kangerlussuaq and Sisimiut, giving information on facilities and services in each town, as well as transport links to and within the towns. As interesting extras, the guide describes two optional ascents at the beginning and end of the route – Sugar Loaf and Nasaasaaq.

The trail itself is described as a hut-to-hut trek, just for the sake of having easily identifiable starting and finishing points for each day. The relevant Greenland Tourism 'Hiking Map' is given in the information box at the start of each day's walk. Tents can be pitched near the huts, or at any suitable point along the trail, and anyone camping will doubtless work to a completely different schedule, which is to be encouraged.

THE ARCTIC CIRCLE TRAIL

A curious scene of shallow water and abundant boulders on the way through Qerrortusup Majoriaa (Day 9)

KANGERLUSSUAQ

Old Camp is the oldest part of Kangerlussuaq, where workers lived while building the US air base

The area north of the fjord of Kangerlussuaq, marked on the Harvey map as the Aasivissuit catchment area, was an important summer reindeer hunting ground, used intermittently by the Inuit from around 200BC. The area still provides good reindeer and musk ox hunting and can be accessed from Hundesø. Kangerlussuaq's history changed forever as a result of World War II and the Cold War. When Hitler's forces invaded Denmark, Henrik Kauffmann, the Danish ambassador in Washington, asked the United States to protect and supply Greenland.

The US military established a number of bases around Greenland,

but Kangerlussuaq was highly favoured as a site for an air base as it enjoyed the most stable weather and clearest skies. On average, there are 300 clear days each year! The base was founded on 7 October 1941, with Colonel Bernt Balchen in command. He was of Norwegian stock and had formerly worked with Amundsen on his polar expeditions.

Under the code name of Bluie West 8 during World War II, the air base was an important link in the supply chain between the US and Allied forces in Europe. Although the base was returned to Denmark in 1950, it again came under US control as part of a new defence pact, reopening as Sondrestrom Air Base, affectionately known as 'Sondy'. During this period, commercial SAS flights made stop-overs on trans-Atlantic routes. The base acquired a civilian presence and became the main airport for visitors to Greenland.

During the Cold War a network of Distant Early Warning (DEW) stations was built across North America. In Greenland they were known as DYE stations (named after Cape Dyer on Baffin Island), and the first was established in 1958. The DYE stations were serviced and supplied from the Sondrestrom Air Base. The Cold War formally ended in 1989, and the DYE stations ceased operations in the early 1990s. US forces withdrew from the Sondrestrom Air Base on 30th September 1992, and the entire site was sold for a mere $10! Since that time the airport has been known by its Greenlandic name of Kangerlussuaq.

The former air base buildings have found new uses as hotels, residences, businesses and shops. A few new buildings have been added, but the whole settlement has a pre-fabricated look about it. Many buildings have old rocket motors outside their doors, as a reminder of past activities. The oldest buildings are at Old Camp, as these were the barrack blocks housing the people who were employed building the air base.

Anyone wanting to delve more deeply into the history of the settlement should visit the Kangerlussuaq Museum. This is open Monday to Saturday 1000–1500, and Sunday by arrangement only. There is an entry fee, tel 84 13 00.

Modern Kangerlussuaq is home to some 500 people who mostly work at the airport, in supporting businesses or in the tourist industry. Naturally, they have health-care facilities, schooling for their children and a range of other services. A transient population of international scientists pass through on their way to study the ice cap, or in earlier years to operate the Incoherent Scatter Radar at the tiny settlement of Kelly Ville.

An 'invasion' of acronyms has accompanied the scientists, and most will spend some time at KISS (Kangerlussuaq International Science Support) while involved with PICO (Polar Ice Coring Office), which has similar aims to GRIP (Greenland Icecore Project), which is easily confused with GISP (Greenland Ice Sheet Project), which all followed on from work originally done by WECO (Western Electric Company) while setting up the DEW and DYE stations.

Of course, those who are walking the Arctic Circle Trail will simply be passing through Kangerlussuaq, maybe pausing only to pick up essential supplies before heading for the wilderness. A surprising range of services and facilities are available, and anyone thinking of extending their trek to include the ice cap will doubtless wish to know more about the settlement.

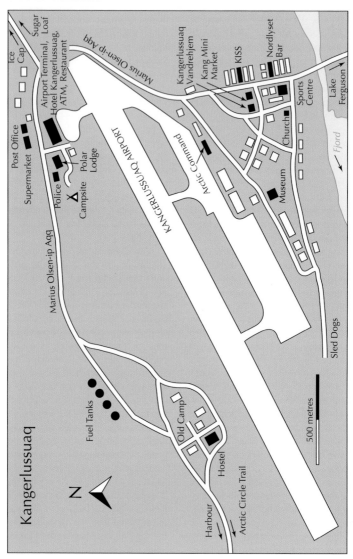

Facilities and services

For all its small size, Kangerlussuaq is currently home to an international airport and is a hub for Air Greenland flights to all parts of the country. Bear in mind that its status could change significantly as new international airports are planned to open in Greenland. Some say that it might be downgraded to a mere heliport. Remember that 'Copenhagen' is rendered as 'København' on departure screens for your return flight.

Kangerlussuaq airport has an ATM, so cash can be obtained on arrival. The airport terminal contains a cafeteria, bar and gift shop. An ice cream shop just outside the airport is an unlikely supplier of gas canisters. The Tele-Post Centre (post office) is across the road from the airport, open Monday to Friday 0900–1100 and 1300–1500. The Pilersuisoq supermarket, which sells gas canisters and other stove fuels, is located alongside. Opening hours are Monday to Thursday 0900–1700, Friday 0900–1800, Saturday 0900–1400 and Sunday 0900–1300. There are also a few gift shops dotted around.

Bear in mind that what you see outside the terminal is only half of the settlement. The other half is reached by turning right and following the 'main' road, Marius Olsenip Aqq, round the end of the airstrip. The Kang Mini Market is a small supermarket with a makeshift café and take-away. Opening hours are Monday to Thursday 1100–1900, Friday and Saturday 1100–2000 and Sunday 1100–1800. The Nordlyset bar offers an odd choice of pizzas and Thai cuisine, with some dishes based on musk ox and reindeer.

In the same part of town is a large sports centre offering a swimming pool (no lifeguard) and a variety of activities; one of the best in Greenland. There is also a separate bowling centre. The Røklubben (rowing club) is out of town, situated by Lake Ferguson, and it incorporates a popular restaurant. For a taste of local produce, try their Greenlandic Buffet on Sundays. Transport along the 5km (3 miles) of dirt road can be arranged when you make a booking. If you want to try cooking local produce yourself, both the supermarkets, as well as the Kangerlussuaq Vandrehjem, sell musk ox and reindeer.

Accommodation

Accommodation options at Kangerlussuaq range from an expensive hotel and a lodge to hostels and a basic campsite. Take note of each option, as well as the route directions to reach them. Be sure to check prices and facilities available at each place, as well as their location on the town plan when making a choice.

Hotels

Those staying at the Hotel Kangerlussuaq simply walk through the airport terminal to find the reception desk and their room. Prices are high, and access to wi-fi is an additional extra, but this is the most

The ice cap near Kangerlussuaq can be visited very easily by taking a bus tour along a dirt road

comfortable place in town. The hotel operates a restaurant and a bar, as well as the reasonably priced airport cafeteria. Luggage storage is available for a fee. Full details and online booking are available, www.hotel kangerlussuaq.gl, tel 84 11 80. Anyone wandering around Kangerlussuaq will notice a rather shabby building called the Hotel Tuttu. This is owned by the Hotel Kangerlussuaq but it is very basic. Its main use is to provide emergency overflow accommodation when flights are delayed or cancelled.

Polar Lodge is located outside the airport terminal, and is reached by turning left and following a wooden walkway. The lodge is in a large hut and offers a number of private rooms with shared toilets and showers, with access to a communal kitchen. Prices are rather high, but include a buffet

breakfast, although wi-fi access is chargeable. There is no luggage storage and guests are advised to use the airport lockers for a fee. Polar Lodge is operated by Albatros Arctic Circle. Full details and online booking are available, albatros-arctic-circle.com/ polar-lodge, tel 84 16 48.

Hostels
There are two hostels available and it is important to distinguish between them as they lie in opposite directions on leaving the airport terminal. Use the town plan of Kangerlussuaq to locate them, because if you ask someone at the airport for directions, they may well send you in completely the wrong direction, and if a taxi takes you the wrong way then it will be a very expensive mistake!

Leave the airport terminal and turn right, following the road called Marius Olsen-ip Aqq all the way around the end of the airstrip. Alternatively, catch the Kangerlussuaq Bybus. Don't turn right along the road signposted for the museum, but turn right along the road that passes the Kang Mini Market. The hostel, or Kangerlussuaq Vandrehjem, is the next building and there is a large sign over its entrance. Operated by Erik and Louise Lomholt-Bek, the hostel provides spacious, comfortable and cheap accommodation throughout the year. Full details and online booking are available, www. kangv.dk. Be sure to check prices and check-in times carefully on the website, as a number of additional services and room upgrades are possible. The most basic price covers a bed in a shared dormitory and access to kitchens, showers, toilets, common room and free luggage storage for the duration of your trek. Higher prices cover private rooms, linen, towels and late check-ins. There is a charge to access wi-fi. There is easy access to the Kang Mini Market and Nordlyset bar and restaurant.

Leave the airport terminal and turn left, following the road out of Kangerlussuaq to Old Camp, where three huts offer hostel accommodation and another hut serves as a reception area and gift shop. Each of the three huts has toilets, showers, kitchen and common room. Prices are rather high, but bus transfer from the airport and a buffet breakfast are included, but remember to bring all other food supplies with you. Luggage storage is not available and wi-fi access is chargeable. The Old Camp hostel is operated by Albatros Arctic Circle. Full details and online booking are available, albatros-arctic-circle. com/old-camp, tel 84 16 48.

Campsite

To find the campsite, leave the airport terminal and turn left. Follow a wooden walkway to Polar Lodge and keep left of the buildings. Eventually, a small blue hut is reached, which is the last building on the edge of town. A toilet and shower are located here, as well as a small room offering shelter in bad weather. A small fee is requested and there are level grassy areas among willow bushes. Dr Frieder Weiße occupies a room in the hut, and with more than a dozen Arctic Circle Trail traverses to his name he can offer up-to-date advice. Frieder also runs the website www. polarrouten.net.

Transport
Bus

The Kangerlussuaq Bybus runs regularly between both halves of Kangerlussuaq, leaving the airport terminal on a regular basis. While the bus can be used to get to and from the Kangerlussuaq Vandrehjem and the museum, it doesn't run to Old Camp. Timetables are posted at bus shelters and bus stops.

Taxi

Taxis can be used to link both halves of Kangerlussuaq quickly, or can be used to get to and from Old Camp. They will also run along nearby dirt roads. Simply pick one up at the airport taxi rank, flag one down on the road, or tel 56 56 56.

Tours

Kang Mini Tours are based at the Kang Mini Market, beside the Kangerlussuaq Vandrehjem. They offer customised tours for small groups, including trips to and from the ice cap, or along the road to Kelly Ville for the start of the Arctic Circle Trail. For full details see www. kangtours.dk, tel 54 01 07.

Albatros Arctic Circle operates from Polar Lodge and Old Camp and run regular trips to and from the ice cap, as well as transporting passengers to and from cruise ships. For full details see albatros-arctic-circle.com, tel 84 16 48.

Ship

Only cruise ships visit the harbour, 14km (8¾ miles) from Kangerlussuaq. There are no ferry services.

Flights

Kangerlussuaq Airport is currently a major hub for Air Greenland flights.

There are daily flights to and from Copenhagen, Sisimiut and other parts of Greenland. However, the permafrost beneath the runway is melting and there are plans to construct new international airports, so in future the status of the airport will be downgraded and the number of flights it will handle will decrease. Check www.airgreenland.com, tel 84 11 42.

Private sightseeing flights operate between Kangerlussuaq and the ice cap. These are expensive and limited to five passengers per flight, with guaranteed window seats. Contact Airzafari, www.airzafari.com, tel 24 85 84.

Websites

Kangerlussuaq and Sisimiut are both part of the municipality of Qeqqata, whose website is available in Danish and Greenlandic at www.qeqqata.gl. The main business interests are represented by Arctic Circle Business and the main tourism interest is Destination Arctic Circle, whose website is available in English, Danish and Greenlandic, destination arcticcircle.com. The official website for the Arctic Circle Trail is arctic circletrail.gl.

PREAMBLE
Ascent of Sugar Loaf

Start/finish	Airport, Kangerlussuaq
Distance	18km (11 miles) there and back
Ascent	500m (1640ft)
Descent	500m (1640ft)
Map	Kangerlussuaq
Terrain	Most of the distance is covered using a broad stony, sandy, dusty dirt road. A short, steep path leads to the summit of the hill.

The Sugar Loaf is a distinctive, steep-sided little hill that even casual visitors to Kangerlussuaq cannot fail to notice. As it stands beside the dirt road leading to the ice cap, many people get to see it at close quarters. An ascent of the Sugar Loaf is easily accomplished from Kangerlussuaq, or it could be included as an 'extra' by anyone walking the dirt road between the ice cap and Kangerlussuaq. The summit is a fine viewpoint.

Ascent of Sugar Loaf

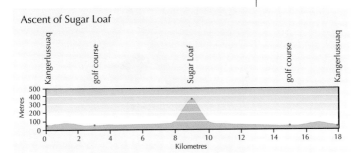

Start from **Kangerlussuaq** by leaving the **airport** and following the main road of Marius Olsen-ip Aqq inland. A junction is reached with a dirt road which is signposted left for the Sugar Loaf, and this is the same road that leads all the way to the ice cap. Follow it uphill and pass an old stone quarry, then drop downhill to the Sondie Arctic

55

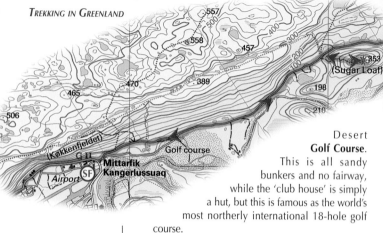

Desert **Golf Course**. This is all sandy bunkers and no fairway, while the 'club house' is simply a hut, but this is famous as the world's most northerly international 18-hole golf course.

Follow the road onwards, passing a junction where another track heads off to the right. The road is flanked by impenetrable willow thickets, along with a few pines bearing metal tags, planted as an experiment to see if

A sign warns motorists on the dirt road to beware of musk oxen – with luck, one might actually be seen

View from the top of the Sugar Loaf, looking down on the grey glacial torrent of Akuliarusiarsuup Kuua

they would thrive. These may be the only real trees you see while you are in Greenland. Later, the road over-looks the dirty grey glacial torrent of **Akuliarusiarsuup Kuua**, which pours from a rocky constriction below the twin summits of the Sugar Loaf.

The road later passes through a 'prohibited' area – a wide circle marked by posts – but passage is allowed along the road. The US military disposed of some dangerous materials in this area, which is occupied by three scenic little lakes and a cabin. Soon after leaving this area, climb up a track on the right and continue up a steep and narrow path. ▸

The slope is covered in willow and birch scrub, with blueberry and crowberry, as well as arctic harebells.

A derelict hut and a few tall wooden masts are all that remains of a communications installation on the hill.

▸ Just beyond is the summit of the **Sugar Loaf,** where a cairn stands on smooth, mineral-veined rock at 353m (1158ft). Views stretch inland to the ice cap, across the grey glacial river to the rugged Akuliarusiarsuk range and Garnet Mountain. Looking beyond Kangerlussuaq to the fjord, the distant Sukkertoppen ice cap can be seen. Westwards lies the terrain traversed by the Arctic Circle Trail – the reason for being here in the first place! Simply retrace your steps to Kangerlussuaq to finish.

A polar bear attacked the personnel stationed at this hut in 1953.

Options for visiting the ice cap

- Walk from Kangerlussuaq to the ice cap and back again (two days with an overnight camp near the ice cap).
- Hire a bicycle at Old Camp and ride to the ice cap and back again (one day and little kit necessary).
- Sign up for a 4WD trip. Either walk or cycle to the ice cap and come back in the vehicle, or travel out in the vehicle and walk or cycle back (as described below). (Bear in mind that 4WD vehicles generally reach the ice cap around 1500, which limits the time for getting back, and an overnight camp might be required.)

OPTIONAL EXTENSION
Ice cap to Kangerlussuaq

Start	'Point 660', ice cap
Alternative start	Russells Glacier
Finish	Airport, Kangerlussuaq
Distance	37km (23 miles) or (alternative start) 25km (15½ miles)
Ascent	340m (1115ft) or 240m (785ft)
Descent	1000m (3280ft) or 700m (2295ft)
Map	Kangerlussuaq
Terrain	A stony, sandy, dusty dirt road. Gradients are mostly gentle and only rarely steep for short stretches. At the ice cap itself, tread warily on both the moraine and the ice.

The dirt road between Kangerlussuaq and the ice cap was constructed for Volkswagen in 2000, so that their cars could be tested in extreme conditions, but it was abandoned soon afterwards. It is now used for 4WD vehicle excursions, giving you the opportunity to extend your trek along the Arctic Circle Trail by starting at the ice cap and walking all the way to Sisimiut. The descent to Kangerlussuaq can be covered at a cracking pace, despite the distance. For those with less time to spare, Russells Glacier offers an alternative start.

Ice cap to Russells Glacier

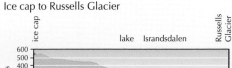
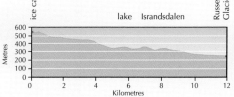

Four-wheel drive vehicles and 'monster truck' buses run from Kangerlussuaq to the so-called **'Point 660'** ▶ where a mass of ill-sorted, frozen, stony moraine hides the ice cap from sight. A path picks its way over this obstacle to reach the very edge of the ice. Specialist equipment is not required to walk on the ice, but tread carefully and don't wander too far as there are dangerous crevasses beyond.

Head back to the dirt road to start walking to Kangerlussuaq, with no route-finding problems for the rest of the day, passing through part of the Aasivissuit – Nipisat World Heritage cultural landscape. ▶ Take the time to admire wildflowers on the grassy slopes, particularly mountain avens. Lakes are a feature of the route, and the first of many is seen down to the right, watered from the edge of the ice cap. Very soon afterwards, a lake full of small icebergs is seen down to the left, where the ice 'calves' directly into the water.

The undulating road passes small lakes and vegetated humps of moraine then drops steeply downhill to cross a bridge over a broad and stony glacial river. Soon afterwards, another bridge is crossed over a short river between two larger lakes. The road rises and falls beside the lake, passing the out-flowing river, which is quickly swallowed into a rocky gorge. Climb uphill to pass through a gap between rocky hills then overlook another lake.

A picnic site is located on the left, on a crest beside the road with toilets below. There are views of a powerful waterfall and the edge of the ice cap. Here, at **Israndsdalen,** the glacier is flanked by a massive lateral

Point 660' is no more than 525m (1720ft) above sea level, but the greater height is always claimed.

The road is used for the Polar Circle Marathon every October. See **www.polar-circle-marathon.com**.

59

At Israndsdalen the ice cap 'calves' small icebergs straight into a river

moraine, and later it 'calves' directly into a river. At other points, water pours from the edge of the ice to augment the flow of the river. The road undulates, but generally heads

Map continues on page 63

down-hill, coming close to the snout of **Russells Glacier.** Here, another picnic site overlooks a powerful, murky grey waterfall. Note the extensive sandbanks deposited here by the river, as well as further downstream.

From Russells Glacier

▶ The road runs more or less level near a lake, where masses of cotton grass grow. Jagged seracs, or ice towers, can be seen above the snout of the glacier. The road reaches a fine viewpoint, marked by a black boulder on the right, overlooking **Aajuitsup Tasia,** or **Long Lake.** This is the largest lake seen from the road, measuring 10km (6¼ miles) in length, at almost 250m (820ft) above sea level.

The road leaves the Aasivissuit – Nipisat World Heritage area and climbs steeply beside a cliff, passing a couple of barrier gates and crossing a gap between the hills at almost 300m (985ft). From this point onwards, willow scrub dominates the slopes, and the distinctive profile of the Sugar Loaf is prominent ahead. The track begins to drop towards the Arctic desert of **Sandflugtdalen.** On the way downhill, note a sandy track heading off to the right, which offers a variant route, described below. This starts with a short, steep climb, then continues easily, offering fine views.

Alternative start: begin walking at Russells Glacier, omitting the first 12km (7½ miles) of the day's walk.

A sandy track leaves the road above Sandflugtdalen and offers an alternative route with better views

At the heart of **Sandflugtdalen** is a glacial river which carries vast quantities of sand and silt downstream. Whenever the flow eases, some of it is deposited to form sandbanks and mudflats. On dry, windy days some of this material, referred to as 'loess', is blown into dust-storms, settling as drifts and dunes. While vegetation can get a root-hold in some parts, it can also be overwhelmed by further drifting. Sandflugtdalen is around 150m (490ft) above sea level. Occasionally, Hercules transporter aircraft practice dropping cargo on the sandflats, preparing for when they have to resupply the Sirius Dog Sled Patrols operating on the ice cap.

Russells Glacier

Metres
500
400
300
200
100
0

0

A grey glacial torrent forms a powerful murky waterfall close to the snout of Russells Glacier

The road undulates beside the sandy valley bottom. The mangled remains of a US aircraft are passed, one of three that crashed in 1968. All the pilots ejected safely. A metal plate bridge is crossed beside mudflats, then another is crossed further along the sandy road. With time to spare, look for animal tracks, including fox, hare, reindeer and musk ox. Tall, tough-stalked lyme grass and broad-leaved willow-herb thrive on the dunes.

The road climbs from the sand and undulates past the scenic little 'Beer Lakes', surrounded by willow scrub. ◀ A track on the left is signposted for Vandfeld, but stay on the road, which crosses a gap beside the steep-sided **Sugar**

US soldiers used to keep beer bottles cool in the lakes while they hiked on their days off.

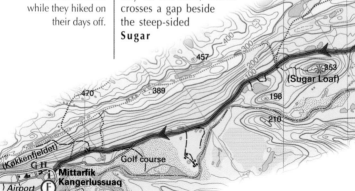

Russells Glacier to Kangelussuaq

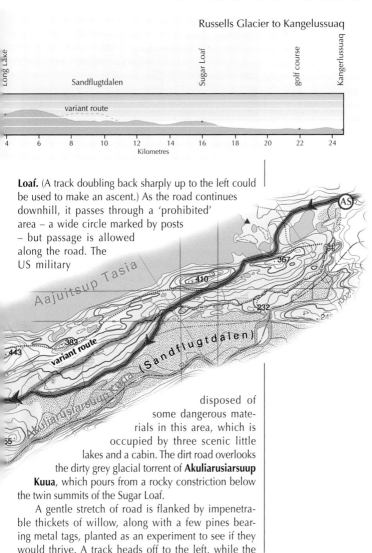

Loaf. (A track doubling back sharply up to the left could be used to make an ascent.) As the road continues downhill, it passes through a 'prohibited' area – a wide circle marked by posts – but passage is allowed along the road. The US military disposed of some dangerous materials in this area, which is occupied by three scenic little lakes and a cabin. The dirt road overlooks the dirty grey glacial torrent of **Akuliarusiarsuup Kuua**, which pours from a rocky constriction below the twin summits of the Sugar Loaf.

A gentle stretch of road is flanked by impenetrable thickets of willow, along with a few pines bearing metal tags, planted as an experiment to see if they would thrive. A track heads off to the left, while the

Sand dumped by a glacial river has blown across Sandflugtdalen to form an arid arctic desert

road continues straight ahead beside the Sondie Arctic Desert **Golf Course**. This is all sandy bunkers and no fairway, while the 'club house' is simply a hut! Follow the road uphill a little, passing an old stone quarry, then later walk downhill to join a tarmac road. Turn right along Marius Olsen-ip Aqq, which is the main road into **Kangerlussuaq**, to finish at the **airport**. Alternatively, turn left along Marius Olsen-ip Aqq if staying at the Kangerlussuaq Vandrehjem.

Variant route

This route starts where a sandy track leaves the road above Sandflugtdalen. There is a steep climb of about 100m (330ft), once used by vehicles, but now badly eroded. Willow scrub grows on either side, and this continues to be the case as the track levels out. On the higher parts, the track is covered in grass, cotton grass and rushes. There are fine views over the valley, taking in the ice cap and the Sugar Loaf. The descent is gentle, dropping around 75m (245ft). The vegetation thins out so that it is mostly sand at the end. Simply rejoin the main route and follow it onwards.

DAY 1

Kangerlussuaq to Hundesø

Start	Airport, Kangerlussuaq
Finish	Hundesø, Kelly Ville
Distance	20km (12½ miles)
Ascent	505m (1655ft)
Descent	335m (1100ft)
Map	Kangerlussuaq
Terrain	Mainly a road walk, rising and falling alongside a tidal fjord. The road has stony and dusty stretches, while the road to Kelly Ville is all stony and dusty.

The first part of the Arctic Circle Trail is along a road. This is obvious and easy, and allows muscles to be flexed after a long flight and backpacks to be adjusted so that they are comfortable to carry. Take the opportunity to study roadside rocks and plants, and they will become easy to identify later. Those who object to road-walking could hire a taxi to Kelly Ville, skipping all but the very last part of this stage.

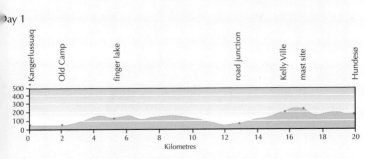

Leave the airport at **Kangerlussuaq** and simply go along the main road called Marius Olsen-ip Aqq. The road passes Polar Lodge, the Politi (police) and the campsite, running level and fringed with vegetation. The airfield lies to the left, while the impressive ice-smoothed rock wall of **Køkkenfjeldet** rises to the right. The wall sheds huge rectangular blocks – one of which has been painted with a mural. When a road junction is reached, Marius Olsen-ip Aqq heads left, while Tankeqarfiup Aqq runs straight ahead past four large fuel tanks. Follow either of these roads as they both join again at **Old Camp**.

This huddle of barrack-style huts called **Old Camp** forms the oldest part of Kangerlussuaq. American servicemen were housed here while building the airport and the rest of the settlement. Three of the huts offer hostel accommodation and all kinds of activities are offered throughout the year.

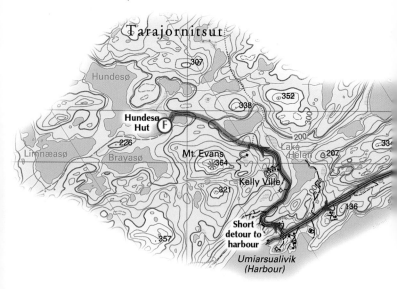

Follow the road called Umiarsualiviup Aqq, which is flanked by yellow barrels as it climbs above the Kangerlussuaq fjord. Maybe take a break at the top of the road, where a picnic bench overlooks the airport runway. Views stretch past Kangerlussuaq to the distinctive dome of the Sugar Loaf, with the ice cap glimpsed beyond. Tasersuatsiaq, or Lake Ferguson, can be seen across the heavily silted fjord.

Take note of the four main **vegetation types** – northern willow, dwarf birch, blueberry and crowberry. These will be seen frequently along the Arctic Circle Trail, each vying for dominance over the others.

There are various tracks and paths running through the rugged strip of land between the road and the sea, but linking them all together to avoid the road-walk is awkward. The road runs downhill in a groove and crosses a narrow finger-lake. Enjoy near and distant views as the road rises and falls, switching from tarmac to a stony, dusty surface and back again. A long

and gradual descent reveals a small portion of the tidal harbour, with the Sukkertoppen ice cap seen in the distance. After passing a big sign for Sondrestrom Port, a road junction is reached beside diesel fuel tanks. A short detour could easily include a visit down to the **harbour**.

The road between Kangerlussuaq and the harbour crosses an attractive narrow finger-lake

Umiarsualivik (the harbour) is a rather bleak, dusty and utilitarian place. There is only a harbour office and a quay, with no facilities of any kind for visitors. When cruise ships dock, their clients are whisked away on buses. One reason for making the detour is to read the colourful graffiti daubed on the cliffs, dating from the arrival of the US military and continuing to the present day.

The road junction is signposted back to the *lufthavn* (airport), 13km (8 miles), and up to Kelly Ville, 3km (2 miles). Follow the broad and dusty dirt road uphill, keeping left to avoid a track leading to a gravel quarry exploiting a massive moraine. Later, keep right to avoid a track serving scattered cabins. Pass behind the massive bank of moraine and follow the road onwards and upwards. ◄ The road overlooks the lovely **Lake Helen** then reaches the former scientific site of **Kelly Ville**.

Two prominent rocks on a hillside were painted by American servicemen, apparently in the form of female breasts. One wonders whether they'd ever seen real ones!

Kelly Ville, also known as Tikilluarit, comprises a huddle of prefabricated huts around a prominent 'incoherent scatter' radar. For many years a small community of scientists studied the ionisation of the upper atmosphere, reducing the natural wonder of the northern lights to mere facts and figures. The facility is now closed and decisions have yet to be made about its future.

Keep climbing up the broad dirt road to reach a junction. The road climbs left towards a building on the slope of **Mount Evans**, but the Arctic Circle Trail runs straight ahead, past the old concrete anchor points of a long-gone communication mast, around 230m (755ft). Study the view ahead, which may include the distant peak of Pingu. There are no longer any views of nearby Kelly Ville and Kangerlussuaq, but a small portion of the ice cap can be seen. ▶

The route is different here as a dirt road now runs all the way to Hundesø.

Walk downhill along a track, confirming your direction by noting a cairn on a boulder on the left, bearing a red paint mark. This is the first marker for the Arctic Circle Trail.

The track leads towards another old concrete anchor point. Keep right of this, and a quad-vehicle track made by reindeer and musk ox hunters runs down a boggy

The first Arctic Circle Trail cairn and paint mark – keep an eye open for the rest on the trek to Sisimiut

Now entering the wilds, the Arctic Circle Trail follows a grassy strip between two lakes at Hundesø

Note that this is the only place to get fresh water for the next 8km (5 miles), as the next few lakes contain brackish water.

slope. This can be followed if desired, but the trail actually runs parallel, just to the left. Either way, head down to a lake and turn left along its shore. ◀ The quad track climbs gently uphill and crosses a broad gap. Descend gently with a view of three lakes ahead. The nearest is nameless, the one beyond is Hundesø, and the one to the left is Brayasø. The Arctic Circle Trail runs along the right-hand shore of the nameless lake then turns left between it and **Hundesø**, passing close to an old caravan.

This is the region of **Tarajornitsut**, which is noted for it slightly brackish lakes. In dry weather, bare patches of earth are crusted with salt, though this vanishes in the rain. Some walkers can't actually taste the salt, while others detect a slight taste. Not everyone would be keen to drink straight from the lakes, but the water is fine if used for cooking or for tea and coffee. Just don't add extra salt!

HUNDESØ HUT

Anyone walking the Arctic Circle Trail without a tent can use an unofficial hut at Hundesø, around 170m (560ft). The 'hut' is actually an old caravan with a couple of sheds attached, tucked behind a hump of rock. It is rather run down, but fine for an overnight stop. The caravan contains bunk beds for four people, a kitchen area, a table, sofa, chairs and a paraffin heater. An adjoining shed contains another bunk bed for two people. The structure is surrounded by wooden decking, for dining outside when mosquitoes allow. A little 'privy' toilet is located in a shed down towards the lake – a loo with a view! The caravan contains all kinds of odds and ends, making some fear they are trespassing in someone's private retreat. It was established by hunters, but there is a guest-book, and the place is regularly used by those walking the Arctic Circle Trail.

DAY 2
Hundesø to Katiffik

Start	Hundesø, Kelly Ville
Finish	Katiffik, Amitsorsuaq
Distance	20km (12½ miles)
Ascent	470m (1540ft)
Descent	520m (1705ft)
Maps	Kangerlussuaq and Pingu
Terrain	An undulating route, though with two distinct ascents and descents. The route passes several lakes, finishing with two large lakes.

Now that the Arctic Circle Trail is properly underway, walkers learn how to look ahead for cairns while following narrow paths that come and go on firm, boggy or rocky ground. Low hummocky hills are passed, and the route runs between them, only once attaining an altitude of 350m (1150ft). The day's walk starts beside a lake, finishes beside a huge lake, and passes several little lakes in between.

Day 2

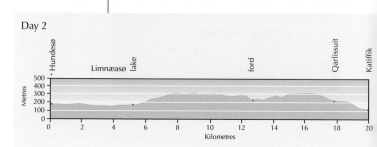

Leave the caravan/hut and head towards the lake of **Hundesø**. If the day is dry, note the salt crusting patches of bare earth. Turn left to follow the shore, where filamentous green algae swirl in the brackish water. A gentle rise separates this lake from **Brayasø**, which is barely glimpsed, if at all. Watch for cairns marking a left turn, gently uphill from the shore of Hundesø, passing a prominent hump of bare rock.

A gentle descent leads back towards a little bay on Hundesø, then head towards the neighbouring lake of **Limnæasø**. ◄ The path keeps away from the shore, rising gently to pass a cairn on bare rock, and descending gently later. Again, if the day is dry, note the salt crust forming on patches of bare ground. The path rises very gently, and there is a little lake to the right. Cross a very broad and gentle gap at almost 200m (655ft) and cross bouldery ground close to a large lake. ◄

Drift to the right, climbing away from the lake for the first real ascent of the day. This is a fairly gentle climb, later levelling out as the path heads for a gap. This is

Don't follow the dirt road running north from Limnæsø. Stay on the Arctic Circle Trail.

This is a freshwater lake, very welcome after the brackish lakes of Tarajornitsut.

curious, as cairns marking the Arctic Circle Trail continue uphill, but there is no path linking them. It appears that walkers are 'voting with their feet' by heading through the gap to see another lake, before climbing uphill to rejoin the cairned route. Be ready to spot little anomalies such as this on the trail.

A prominent cairn is reached, over 300m (985ft), where a lake containing a small island is seen ahead. Stay high on the slope. The path is clear and there are cairns. Further ahead, a huddle of prominent domed hills is seen, which the route reaches towards the end of the day. The path passes a few small lakes, mostly circular, and on a clear day a distant peak might be noticed – Pingu – which will dominate views in days to come. It can be spotted a couple more times during this day, always on the right, framed by gaps in the hills.

The path undulates gently before dropping quite distinctly to reach a small, level area of boggy ground between two lakes. This is marked as a **tent pitch** on the map. The large lake to the right is Qarlissuit, which will be seen frequently during the rest of the day. First, a narrow river needs to be forded between the two

The lakeshore of Qarlissuit, before the descent to the Katiffik Hut and Amitsorsuaq

KATIFFIK HUT

This hut is rather small and dark, having only one window. It is simply one small room, with a sleeping platform for three people, although three more could sleep on the floor beneath. There is a fixed bench and a small table, as well as a small cooking area. A storage shed is built into the side of the hut. A canoe frame stands beside the lake. If there are canoes on it, these can be used to cover tomorrow's route. First check that they are watertight and have the necessary paddles and lifejackets.

lakes. Sometimes this is barely noticeable, but at other times it needs to be waded and could be knee-deep.

Once across, climb steeply a short way, keeping left of a little hill.

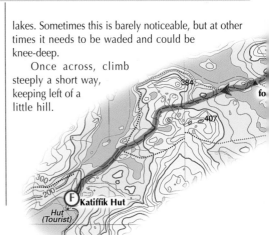

Drop down to another gap with a low hump on it, still with the same two lakes on either side. Climb again, this being the second real ascent of the day. The path reaches the domed hills seen earlier and passes between them. After crossing a dip and climbing to around 350m (1150ft), there is one final opportunity to look back and catch a glimpse of the distant ice cap.

Another path climbs along a rounded crest, but if followed it becomes awkward to continue.

The path undulates gently, passing a bouldery brow overlooking two small, round boggy pools. Walk downhill across a boggy dip, with a view of Qarlissuit down to the right and Amitsorsuaq beyond it. Climb again, but when the path descends, keep right to head down to the shore of **Qarlissuit**, landing near a small sandy beach around 230m (755ft). ▶

Walk along the lake shore and head straight through a gap as marked by a cairn. Follow a path down a

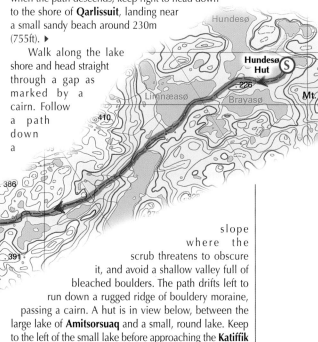

slope where the scrub threatens to obscure it, and avoid a shallow valley full of bleached boulders. The path drifts left to run down a rugged ridge of bouldery moraine, passing a cairn. A hut is in view below, between the large lake of **Amitsorsuaq** and a small, round lake. Keep to the left of the small lake before approaching the **Katiffik Hut**, around 120m (395ft).

75

DAY 3
Katiffik to Canoe Centre

Start	Katiffik, Amitsorsuaq
Finish	Canoe Centre, Amitsorsuaq
Distance	20km (12½ miles)
Ascent	200m (665ft)
Descent	200m (665ft)
Map	Pingu
Terrain	A lakeshore walk, with a couple of awkward boulder slopes. There are short detours from the shore to avoid small cliffs rising from the water and little headlands. This stage can be covered using a canoe, if one is available at Katiffik.

This entire day features the splendid large lake of Amitsorsuaq, around 120m (395ft) above sea level, and there are two ways to cover the distance. Either walk along the southern shore or paddle along the lake in a canoe. The walk is fairly straightforward, with no route-finding difficulties, though there are a couple of rugged boulder slopes soon after starting. Those who wish to paddle along the lake rely entirely on someone having come the other way and left their canoe at Katiffik. A new fleet of canoes was put in place in 2022. Treat them with respect and do not damage or abandon them.

Day 3

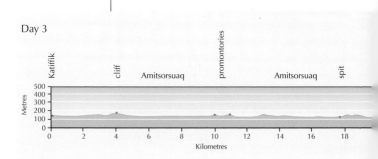

The walking route

Leave the **Katiffik Hut** and follow the lakeshore path round the head of **Amitsorsuaq**, where there is a sandy beach. An easy path hugs the shore, but later crosses a steep and boulder-studded slope. At one point huge boulders litter the slope, and the path is forced closer to the shore. Watch for paint marks on two big boulders, where it is almost necessary to step into the water to pass them.

Continue across another steep slope to reach an even more awesome slope of massive boulders. These angular blocks are piled on top of each other, and some have tumbled far into the lake. There are bits of trodden path, often hidden by clumps of willow. Stay as low as possible to wriggle between the boulders. There is nothing to be gained by climbing high up the slope. Look in dark recesses to spot colonies of ferns.

The path continues easily towards a headland jutting into the lake. Don't go to the end of the point, but shortcut over a low-slung gap instead. The path passes to the left of a small pond, which is separated from the lake only by a narrow sandy beach. Another bouldery slope is too difficult to negotiate, so the path climbs high above a rugged cliff. ▶

A tall cairn marks a slight detour away from the shore of Amitsorsuaq

Cairns marking the Arctic Circle Trail cross a gap behind the cliff, but walkers have trodden a higher path.

From the top of the cliff, views extend to the glaciated peaks of Aqqutikitsoq, north of Sisimiut. Head downhill, and the path gradually becomes easier along the lake shore. An island lies across the lake, looking remarkably rugged considering it rises only around 75m (245ft) above the water, peaking at 194m (636ft). Keep an eye on its summit while following the path, because in fine weather the twin peaks of Pingup Sallia and Pingu can be seen far beyond it. These peaks dominate distant views for the next couple of days.

A very definite right turn is made around a bay, passing a scrap of sandy beach. Climb past a couple of smooth, rounded, split rocky outcrops. This is marked as a **tent pitch** on the map. The path continues easily, close to the shore, with views of dramatically contorted cliffs either side of the island. Later, the path shortcuts behind two little peninsulas, though it is worth climbing onto them for fine views. One is marked as a **tent pitch** on the map. Further along the lake shore, be ready for a gentle climb away from the water, which many walkers miss, as they don't notice a small cairn above the shore. (A very tall cairn has been built at one point, which despite looking unstable, has survived for many years.)

Look across the lake to spot a dramatic fold in the rock at the base of a cliff. The

path runs downhill and continues easily along the shore. Note how many boulders poke above the shallow water along this stretch. Further on, don't go out onto a point marked as a tent pitch on the map, as the point ends with a hooked spit, and steps would have to be retraced. Instead, the Arctic Circle Trail climbs above the lake to avoid a couple of little cliffs ahead, and the Canoe Centre can be seen ahead for the first time, as well as a rocky little islet closer to hand. When the path returns to the shore, it remains easy all the way to the **Canoe Centre**.

The canoe route

Those hoping to paddle along Amitsorsuaq can pick up a canoe at the **Katiffik Hut**, as long as someone else has come the other way and left one there. If there is a canoe waiting on the frame, make sure that you inspect the hull, paddles and lifejackets. Test the canoe in the water, then load it evenly for stability. The canoes are designed to carry two people and their kit to a maximum of 400kg (880lb). Ideally, two people should paddle. It is possible for one person to do it alone, but it can be very difficult to maintain a direct line. A new fleet of canoes was put in place in 2022. Do not damage them, or lose the paddles and lifejackets. Never abandon a canoe

It is recommended to stay fairly close to the shore, where the clear water allows you to see the lake bed. By staying close to the southern shore, you can keep an eye on the walking route, maybe taking a close look at the bouldery slopes soon after starting. For those paddling along the northern shore, there are

79

A fleet of canoes is available on the lake of Amitsorsuaq, but if using one, never abandon it

If a break is needed at any time, try to come ashore on sandy beaches, for the sake of the canoe hull.

fine views of rugged cliffs. Once a large island has been passed, peaking at 194m (636ft), bear in mind that the water along the southern shore is quite shallow and there are several boulders poking above it. ◄

Naturally, progress depends on weather conditions. A good easterly breeze is ideal for the trip, while a westerly wind makes it more difficult, the stronger it blows. Do not abandon a canoe unless you really have no option. If you do have to abandon one, please leave it well above the southern shore in a place where it can be seen both from the lake and the path, so that it can be retrieved easily by someone else. Every year there are fewer canoes left, probably because people carelessly abandon them in places where they eventually get lost or sink.

After turning a point and passing a rugged little islet, the **Canoe Centre** is in view and is quickly reached. Pull the canoe out of the water onto the land above the beach. Turn it upside down and ensure that the paddles and life-jackets are secured. If not staying at the Canoe Centre, then it is possible to paddle the canoe all the way to the foot of the lake.

CANOE CENTRE

The Canoe Centre is the largest hut along the Arctic Circle Trail, though 'hut' is too mean a word for the building. It stands above a sandy beach, around 120m (395ft), and boasts two dormitories, each with enough bunk beds for eight people. One of the dormitories has a paraffin heater. There is a large kitchen/dining room, with a table and benches, and beds for six more people, as well as another paraffin heater. Several more people could sleep on the floor. There are also two toilets just inside the entrance. A large shed, accessed from outside the building, is used as a canoe store and workshop.

Solar panels were installed in 2022, which convert sunlight into electrical power throughout the long summer days, which is stored in batteries. Trekkers can recharge their devices at this stage on the trail. Treat this facility with respect, because if anyone breaks it, repairs won't be made swiftly.

DAY 4
Canoe Centre to Ikkattooq

Start	Canoe Centre, Amitsorsuaq
Finish	Ikkattooq
Distance	22km (13½ miles)
Ascent	650m (2130ft)
Descent	450m (1475ft)
Map	Pingu
Terrain	A lakeshore path gives way to a gentle walk down through a valley to another lake. The trail climbs into rugged mountains, with some short, steep sections. The undulating route passes several little lakes. Careful navigation is required in mist, especially where there is no trodden path on bare rock.

After following the last part of the shoreline path on Amitsorsuaq, the Arctic Circle Trail follows the outflowing river down to another lake. This lake, Kangerluatsiarsuaq, seems large but is merely a bay on the much bigger lake of Tasersuaq. In fine weather, a bright, sandy beach lapped by blue water proves to be a great distraction. The route climbs into a rugged mountain range, and although the path is generally good, it could be lost in mist. There is a little hut the mountains, the highest on the trail, around 320m (1050ft).

Leave the **Canoe Centre** and walk along the shore of Amitsorsuaq. A small lake lies close to the large lake, and the route passes between them. In fine weather, views ahead include the prominent mountain of Pingup Sallia. Nearby slopes were burnt in 2017 and the vegetation will take decades to recover. As the end of the lake is reached, the path passes a **canoe frame**. Lake views are attractive, with lots of boulders projecting from the shallow water. (Anyone paddling a canoe as far as the western end of the lake should leave it here. Drag the canoe carefully out of the water and turn it upside down on the frame. Secure the paddles and lifejackets for the next user.)

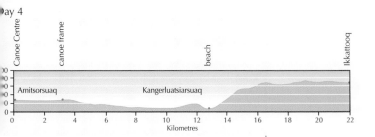

Follow the outflowing river downstream. The Arctic Circle Trail officially crosses the river, passes a couple of prominent cairns on a bouldery rise, and crosses the river again. However, walkers have trodden a path keeping left of the river, without crossing, even though it means walking through a boggy patch. Use the trodden path and simply follow the river, gradually pulling away from it and watching for cairns along the way. At some unmarked point, the trail enters the Aasivissuit – Nipisat World Heritage cultural landscape, passing through it for the next two days.

There are fine views down towards a lake, with mountains beyond. Cross old mudflows, now solid and vegetated, with boggy patches in between. The path is like a miniature roller-coaster, with lots of little ups and

Trekkers take a break before the descent to Kangerluatsiarsuaq

downs, but the general trend is downhill towards the lake, finally crossing a gravelly mound containing broken shells. A peak to the east, rising to 360m (1181ft), has an attractive rocky face.

Turn left to follow the path above the lake shore of **Kangerluatsiarsuaq**. The path climbs steadily, but could be lost on the ascent. It crosses a gap beside a low rocky hill, where a peninsula juts out into the lake. This is marked as a **tent pitch** on the map. Drop steeply downhill on the other side, landing near a remarkable sandy beach. On a sunny day, this is a stunningly scenic location. The beach slopes gently into the water, forming a linear bank effectively damming a small pool, with Pingu rising to the north. Rather surprisingly, the lake level is less than 25m (80ft) above sea level.

Walk round the back of the pool to pick up a path. This becomes

better trodden as it climbs, passing a cairn on a prominent boulder above a vegetated slope. Lying ahead are three rugged cliffs. The path climbs the first of these, which is low and easy, with an old mudflow beyond. The next two climbs are short, steep and rugged. The gradient eases afterwards, while the path undulates and writhes through a landscape of rugged humps and bumps. Enjoy intriguing views over Kangerluatsiarsuaq and the huge Tasersuaq, which sometimes look like three separate lakes. Closer to hand are small, shallow mountain lakes, some of which dry out completely in the summer. Keep an eye on the path and cairns, especially in mist. The altitude reaches 350m (1150ft) near a slope of bare rock.

IKKATTOOQ HUT

This little hut is located on a broad and rugged gap, around 320m (1050ft), overlooking an attractive lake. It is rather like a garden shed, and consists of one room, with bunks sleeping six people, a fixed bench, a small cooking area and a paraffin heater. Water is available from the nearby lake, which drains into the larger lake of Ikkarluttooq. Please bear in mind that snowmobiles do not visit this hut in the winter, so leave absolutely nothing behind and do not attempt to get rid of rubbish by burning it.

The route descends gradually into a valley filled with small, interconnected lakes, somewhat larger than the little lakes passed elsewhere on the way through this hum-mocky mountain range. Look towards the head of the valley, where there is a broad and rugged gap. The Ikkattooq Hut might be spotted, though it is not easy to distinguish from a distance. However, the trodden path leads all the way to the door of the hut. The land around the hut was burnt in 2016 and the vegetation will take decades to recover.

On a fine day the beach beside Kangerluatsiarsuaq would not look out of place in the Mediterranean!

DAY 5
Ikkattooq to Eqalugaarniarfik

Start	Ikkattooq
Finish	Eqalugaarniarfik
Distance	11km (7 miles)
Ascent	330m (1080ft)
Descent	520m (1705ft)
Map	Pingu
Terrain	Mountainous at first, with an intermittent path, so take careful note of cairns, especially on a long, steep and rocky descent. There is a choice of routes across low-lying bog, depending on whether a river is in flood. The final part is along a firm, easy path.

Although the route is already high in the mountains, there are a number of ascents and descents before a steep and rocky descent to the river of Itinneq. Before landing in the valley, spend time studying the view, noting the layout of the river, the large and small pools flanking it, and the vegetation cover. Normally, a path can be followed straight to the river for a simple knee-deep ford. If the river is in flood, then a footbridge is available, but it has to be reached by making a long, arduous, pathless walk along the boggy valley floor. A good path finally leads to a fine hut.

Leave the **Ikkattooq Hut** and follow the path across a little dip. A short, but steep climb leads to a little pool that might be completely dry. The path swings right to climb and traverse a steep and rocky slope. Note how the rock breaks into rectangular blocks that fall and litter the slope beneath. Further uphill, turn left to pass prominent cairns on a rocky edge. There are fine views back to the hut and the many lakes near it, as well as southwards to the distant Sukkertoppen ice cap beyond the unseen fjord of Kangerlussuaq.

The path crosses a dip, and there is a little lake down to the left. After a steep climb, another lake lies to the right. Climb above it, passing a succession of smooth, rounded

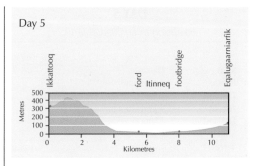

Day 5

outcrops of rock, liberally scattered with large stones and boulders. Naturally, the path comes and goes in this sort of terrain, so keep looking ahead to spot cairns. The route comes close to a summit at 448m (1470ft), but crosses a gentle dip where another little lake lies to the left.

When a high vantage point is reached, views stretch across the valley of the Itinneq, or Ole's Lakseelv, with the mountains of Pingup Sallia and Pingu seen across a small part of the enormous lake of Tasersuaq. Throughout the descent, remember to keep watching for cairns, as the route often crosses smooth and gentle whaleback humps of rock, many strewn with boulders. Watch for the route changing direction on the descent, while being drawn towards a rocky little valley. The route doesn't enter the valley, but swings left to go down smooth ribs of rock,

heading straight for the low-lying, broad-floored valley of the **Itinneq**, or **Ole's Lakseelv**, where the Arctic Circle Trail encounters its widest and deepest river. At the foot of the slope, a decision needs to be made as to whether to ford the river.

Descending from the hills into a broad valley drained by the Itinneq

The river is likely to be at its deepest and swiftest during the thaw, early in June. As the summer wears on, its flow decreases, unless boosted by unusually heavy rainfall. There is a suitable fording point in the river, where the water is usually chest-deep and very cold in June, less than waist deep in July, and less than knee-deep in August. In July 2007 a footbridge was installed 2.5km (1½ miles) from the ford, as the crow flies. This should be used only if the ford is impassable (which will be a matter of personal judgement, dependent on skills and experience), since there is no trodden path to the bridge, and anyone trying to take advantage of the bridge will find themselves seriously disadvantaged by the terrain.

To allow a comparison, the 'main route' and 'flood route' are described separately.

The author demonstrates the ford on the Itinneq, or Ole's Lakseelv, which is the biggest river crossed on the whole trail

If conditions are unsuitable for a crossing, retrace your steps and follow the 'flood route'. Don't be tempted to follow the river downstream, as it is far too bendy. If boats are moored nearby, they belong to hunters and should not be touched. The GPS co-ordinates for the ford are 66.992402 -52.270477.

Main route (with river crossing)

A path leads straight across the broad and boggy floor to the **Itinneq**, or **Ole's Lakseelv**. The wettest part is on grass and cotton grass, then drier ground is covered in erect birch scrub. There is a signpost suggesting that this is the way to both the river and the bridge. Pass a broad area of mud and stones, which is hopefully dry and firm, but it might be covered by shallow water. When the river is reached, a cairn can be seen on the opposite bank. However, it is usually best to cross a little upstream, where the water is shallower. Early in the summer it can be chest-deep, while late in the summer it is barely knee-deep. ◄

Once across, head for a rock wall and turn left. A pool of water abuts the rock, so climb a little and traverse the face, then continue along a boggy path. Stay at the very edge of the valley, where the broad boggy floor meets the steep sides, and where there is often a sloping rock wall. Eventually, after a very wet bog, cairns take the route gently up from the valley floor onto a rounded rocky crest overlooking the valley. Along this stretch, the 'main route' is joined by 'flood route'.

Flood route (via bridge)

Quite honestly, if you are considering this route purely to save getting your feet wet, then it isn't worth the trouble. This route should be followed **only** if the ford is impassable, for reasons that will become clear. First, there is no path, and no markers of any sort. The route simply forges straight westwards along the broad and boggy floor to the **Itinneq**, or **Ole's Lakseelv**. The most awkward part comes first, where two small sluggish streams have to be crossed in soft and deep bog. Next, the route keeps right of a couple of large pools, then keeps right of a rocky spur projecting from the mountains into the valley.

On drawing level with the spur, look carefully for a slight mound that is higher than the surrounding bog, and while walking along it, watch for a huddle of boulders embedded in it. Keep walking across the valley to find the river, which isn't easy to spot as it lies deeply entrenched. Once located, follow it downstream to find the footbridge. ▸

Cross over, then head for a low rock wall ahead, finding a breach in it to climb uphill. A narrow path is

On the map, the bridge is exactly where the 52° 20′ line crosses the river, or if you use a GPS to locate it, the co-ordinates are 66.988044 -52.334833

A bridge too far? Many walkers who aim for this bridge wish that they had forded the river instead!

reached, which is the Arctic Circle Trail 'main route'. Turn left to follow it.

The path climbs gently, either along the rounded rocky crest or along a gently sloping strip of bog. Either way, the route climbs above the valley floor and later overlooks the tidal head of the fjord called **Maligiaq**. The path swings right as it climbs gently, passing beneath a chunky rocky peak. Keep looking ahead to spot the **Eqalugaarniarfik Hut**, standing at 130m (425ft).

EQALUGAARNIARFIK HUT

This fine hut overlooks the tidal head of Maligiaq, one of a handful of small fjords leading into a much broader fjord. The view is charming, and changes with the ebb and flow of the tide. There is a large kitchen/diner/bedroom, with a paraffin heater. There are two sleeping platforms, with room for two or three people on each side. Any more would have to sleep on the floor. There is also a toilet and a small vestibule store. Ideally, you should carry water to the hut, otherwise it needs to be brought from the valley below the hut, or from further along the trail. Small boats from the nearby village of Sarfannguit and the more distant town of Sisimiut occasionally reach the head of the fjord. If a rapid exit from the trail is required, it might be possible to negotiate a passage with the crew.

DAY 6

Eqalugaarniarfik to Innajuattoq

Start	Eqalugaarniarfik
Finish	Innajuattoq
Distance	19km (12 miles)
Ascent	680m (2230ft)
Descent	510m (1675ft)
Maps	Pingu and Sisimiut
Terrain	On the initial ascent the trail is tangled up with a bulldozed track, so watch carefully for cairns. A high, rounded, rocky crest is followed before the trail passes a series of interesting interconnected lakes in a scenic valley.

This is a day of mountains and lakes. The mountains are fairly easy to climb, and the highest part is an undulating rocky crest around 450m (1475ft). From it, views take in a series of splendid lakes, with higher mountains rising beyond. The Arctic Circle Trail wanders beside a few of these lakes, and the day's walk finishes beside a further charming lake. There is a choice of two huts for the night – a small and simple structure on a little hilltop, or a larger and more spacious building closer to the lake.

Leave the **Eqalugaarniarfik Hut** and follow a path to a bouldery riverbed. This is sometimes dry and sometimes full of water. A lake lying directly to the north was dammed in 2007, so only if the dam overflows is there water present. Immediately after crossing the riverbed, there is a bulldozed track, an eyesore, which was made to convey heavy equipment from the head of the fjord up to the lake in order to construct the dam.

Avoid this track as much as possible, first by crossing it, then by looking for cairns marking the Arctic Circle Trail, which runs slightly higher than the track. The trail joins the track later, and the track is followed up to a sudden left bend. Step off the track at this point and follow a narrow, undulating path across a slope. ▶ There

A dirt road is joined on this stage, which runs all the way to Sisimiut. A more southerly trail avoids most of the road, but it hasn't yet been checked for this guidebook.

Day 6

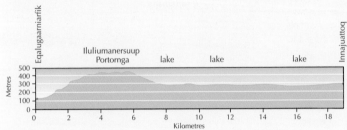

Domed mountains with steep rocky faces are seen to good effect during the initial ascent of the day

are fine views across the valley towards domed mountains with sheer cliff faces. When the trail joins the track again, climb steeply for a short way to reach a cairn on a rounded outcrop then abandon the track. The track continues off-route to a small dam around 300m (985ft). Water from lakes to the east has been diverted through lakes to the west, augmenting the flow to a distant hydro-electric power station.

As soon as the track drops downhill, head off to the left to follow a narrow path. Keep watching for cairns to cross a small valley and climb onto a rounded, rocky crest, then turn left along it. One of the first summits is crowned with an immense boulder that has split into huge chunks. Nearby expanses of bare rock are liberally strewn with boulders.

This is all part of the sprawling upland of **Iluliumanersuup Portornga**, and the general altitude is around 450m (1475ft). The crest undulates, and some parts are crumbling to sand and grit. Views are exceptional, featuring a truly dazzling string of large and small lakes wrapped around the foot of the Taseeqqap Saqqaa range. The mountains may bear snow patches, while a

(map labels: 407 · dam · Iluliumanersuup Portornga · 639 · 596 · bulldozed track · Eqalugaarniarfik Hut · S · Polar Route · footbridge · Itinneq)

Map continues on page 97

Lakes and mountains are seen throughout the day

distant view through a valley may reveal the glacial peaks of Qaqapalat.

It is important to watch carefully for cairns, especially before a steep descent of 100m (330ft) or so, during which a small lake, then a larger lake, are passed. A narrow path picks its way along the southern shore of the lake or climbs to avoid a small cliff rising from the water. Steep, north-facing cliffs often prevent direct sunlight at this end of the lake. Plants growing here are adapted to low light.

The route begins to swing northwards, climbing gently to cross a stream and overlook a small lake. This is marked as a **tent pitch** on the map. Pass a cairn and drop down towards a much larger lake, crossing another stream on the way. The lake shore is around 300m (985ft), and while the map suggests a level shoreline walk, the path actually rises and falls several times and is often some distance from the water. Sometimes it passes through boggy patches, stony patches or areas of dense willow scrub. ◄

A higher path has evolved, which might be followed instead of the shoreline path.

Most walkers follow the shore until a river flows out of the lake, which they then follow downstream. However, before reaching the outflow, cairns might be noticed on humps of moraine and bare rock above the lake. There is a path crossing a rise and cairns are painted with Arctic Circle Trail markers. Either way, a path leads onwards down through a broad valley, where the river often splits into channels before entering a lake. The ground flanking the lake is tussocky, wet and boggy, and the narrow path is some distance from the shore. Great slabby cliffs rise to rounded mountain tops.

As the river leaves the lake it splits into channels, many of which form broad, shallow pools, while lazy meanders sidle through a broad boggy area. After joining another river, the water heads lazily northwards. Fortunately, walkers do not need to cross any of these rivers, or the bog, and the path simply keeps to the foot of a slope where the ground is firm and dry.

Looking ahead up a broad valley, a rounded hill can be seen, and a little hut is perched just to the left of its summit. Some walkers head straight towards this, across

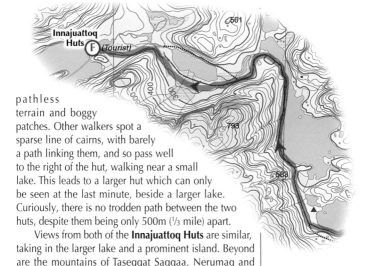

pathless
terrain and boggy
patches. Other walkers spot a
sparse line of cairns, with barely
a path linking them, and so pass well
to the right of the hut, walking near a small
lake. This leads to a larger hut which can only
be seen at the last minute, beside a larger lake.
Curiously, there is no trodden path between the two
huts, despite them being only 500m (⅓ mile) apart.

Views from both of the **Innajuattoq Huts** are similar,
taking in the larger lake and a prominent island. Beyond
are the mountains of Taseqqat Saqqaa, Nerumaq and
Innajuattoq. Looking back through the valley, away from
the lake, are the Igannaq and Taseeqqap Saqqaa ranges.
All the higher mountains, over 1000m (3280ft), have
small but permanent snow patches.

INNAJUATTOQ HUTS

The little hut on the hill,
around 300m (985ft), is a
cosy, one-roomed affair,
with a window, but note
how it is lashed down by
cables in case it blows
away! There is a sleeping
platform for three people,
with room for three more
on the floor beneath. A
small fixed bench and
table are available, along
with a small cooking area

and a paraffin heater. The hut is perched above a lovely sandy beach, where water can be obtained from the lake.

The splendid larger building by the lake deserves a better name than 'hut' – maybe something like 'The Lake House'. It stands at around 275m (900ft). An earlier structure burnt down in April 2008, but it was promptly  replaced with this new model. It has a spacious kitchen/dining room with a paraffin heater. A dormitory sleeps 10 people in bunk beds, with another paraffin heater. There is also a toilet and a small vestibule store room. Water is available either from the lake or from a nearby river.

DAY 7
Innajuattoq to Nerumaq

Start	Innajuattoq
Finish	Nerumaq
Distance	17km (10½ miles)
Ascent	370m (1215ft)
Descent	520m (1705ft)
Map	Sisimiut
Terrain	Apart from an initial gentle climb from a lake, the route is mostly downhill, passing fairly easily through a valley flanked by mountains.

This is a fairly simple and straightforward day. A gentle ascent offers great views back across the lake to the steep and rugged flanks of the Taseeqqap Saqqaa range. While crossing a couple of easy gaps, views southwards take in the broad crest of Taseqqat Saqqaa, with Nerumaq closer to hand. An easy walk down through a scenic valley ends with an abrupt change of direction, where the next hut is seen quite suddenly. Strong walkers might consider walking further down through the valley to the next hut, but the additional 17km (10½ miles) can make the whole day's walk seem very long and tiring.

Day 7

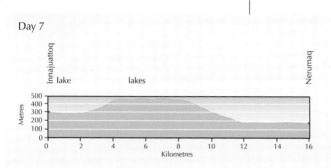

Leave the small or large **Innajuattoq Hut** and cross the river flowing from the lake. This is usually easiest at the point where the water leaves the lake, and can be done by hopping from boulder to boulder, though some may prefer to wade. Just a short distance downstream the river pours into a rocky gorge where fording is not recommended. However, it becomes easier to ford below the gorge.

After crossing, simply follow a lakeshore path through low willow scrub. Later, there is a boggy patch to negotiate, then the path gradually pulls away from the lake.

Climb gently up a slope, crossing a couple of little streams while weaving through tall and springy willow. There are a few narrow paths, so keep an eye open for cairns and aim for a little gap on the southern slopes of Innajuattoq. Cairns on top of prominent boulders help with general route-finding. There is a small lake down to the left, then, after crossing a squelchy patch of cotton grass, a bouldery stretch leads past a smaller lake, which

Looking back towards the lake with the rugged Taseeqqap Saqqaa range rising beyond

lies to the right. Remember to keep looking back during the ascent, as splendid views unfold.

The path continues across a bouldery slope and passes a cairn above a gap, around 475m (1560ft). There is only a slight descent, then the path roughly contours across a steep slope, entering a long, shallow groove that is rather like a small valley suspended high above a deeper valley nearby. Interesting little flowers adorn south-facing slopes. Keep to the right of a little lake, then look left across a few larger lakes towards the Taseqqat Saqqaa range, which holds permanent snow patches. Pass another lake, somewhat larger and curved, and again keep to the right of it. Climb towards another gap, around 475m (1560ft), then climb above a cairn on the gap, as the path does.

Walk downhill, still in a small valley, but when a tussocky bog is reached look out for a cairn and watch carefully for the continuation of the path, which now slips down across a slope into the main valley, below the slopes of **Nerumaq**. ▶ The walk down into the valley is simple and relatively easy. The ground is well vegetated, with a clear path and very few boulders. Cross a stream and follow the path gently up onto a little hill made of stony moraine, capped by a cairn. The river below looks attractive, though it winds through an awkward tussocky bog. A prominent humped buttress rises opposite.

The path stays on a sort of shelf lying at the foot of a steep slope, but at the same time perched high above the river. The shelf is made of sand, gravel and stones – essentially glacial moraine that has slumped from the steep valley sides to become consolidated and vegetated. Be thankful for it, since it provides a firm, dry, easy surface for walking.

The valley begins to swing right beneath a steep slope, passing

Some trekkers miss the cairn and follow a more rugged path on a parallel course, but this eventually joins the correct path further downhill.

several large boulders. Looking across the valley, a steep and rocky slope may be in complete shadow if it is seen late in the day. A small lake lies to the left, while ahead are rugged mountainsides and possibly even a glimpse of the glaciated peaks of Aqqutikitsoq. A signpost is reached where the Arctic Circle Trail drops to ford a river. The **Nerumaq Hut** used to stand at this point. For some reason it was dragged to a new location a few hundred metres away, but it is clearly in view.

NERUMAQ HUT

This hut stands on the level valley floor at around 150m (490ft), flanked by steep rocky mountains rising to 835m (2740ft). These effectively block out the sunlight in the evening, so that even in summer it can get a bit chilly. The hut is rather like a garden shed, and consists of one room with bunks sleeping six people, a fixed bench, a small cooking area and a paraffin heater. It is

painted white inside, so it only takes a little light to brighten the place, but it is also one of the shabbiest huts on the trail. Water is available from the nearby river, which is full of Arctic char, or from a nearby tributary.

DAY 8
Nerumaq to Kangerluarsuk Tulleq

Start	Nerumaq
Finish	Kangerluarsuk Tulleq
Distance	16 or 17km (10 or 10½ miles) depending on choice of hut
Ascent	200 or 300m (655 or 985ft)
Descent	325m (1065ft)
Map	Sisimiut
Terrain	Essentially a low-level valley walk, but there are patches of dense willow scrub, river crossings and squelchy bog to negotiate. In poor weather all these would prove very tiring. There is either a level walk to one hut or a climb to the other at the end of the day.

On the map, this looks like a simple valley walk, and in fine weather it poses no real problems. In wet weather, walking through dense willow scrub could cause a soaking. During the early thaw, or after heavy rain, the three river crossings could prove awkward. After a dry spell the river can be waded easily, or boulder-hopped dry-shod. The lower parts of the valley are usually wet and boggy. At the day's end there is a choice of huts – one at the head of the fjord of Kangerluarsuk Tulleq and one lying further uphill.

Day 8

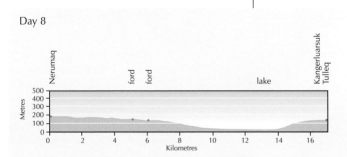

Leave the **Nerumaq Hut** and retrace steps to the signpost before fording the river. This can often be achieved by boulder-hopping. Walk downstream and take the time to look back across the valley at the steep rocky mountains with massive boulder screes below them. The path passes more big boulders then reaches a wet and boggy patch. After

A river is followed downstream from the Nerumaq Hut, crossing boggy ground and passing willow scrub

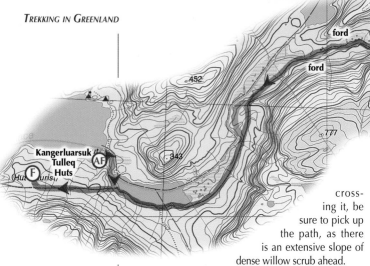

crossing it, be sure to pick up the path, as there is an extensive slope of dense willow scrub ahead.

Walk slowly through the willow thickets, always watching for the narrow and stony path, taking care while stepping on springy, slippery branches underfoot. Keep looking for cairns, and take special note of the prominent ones on top of boulders, which help with general route-finding. The path often runs well away from the river, and if it is lost, it can prove difficult to locate again.

Eventually, the path runs down to the river, where a rock bar provides a natural ford, just before the river is swallowed into a bouldery gorge. When the river is low, it may be possible to boulder-hop across nearby. The path continues downstream, between the river and a slope of rock that is crumbling to sand and grit. Not far downstream, cairns mark the position of another ford, and again, it may be possible to boulder-hop across nearby.

Keep walking downstream, and the path generally drifts away from the river and is sometimes located high above the broad and stony flow. The map later indicates that the route climbs over a spur around 100m (330ft), but the trodden path runs close to the river. Obviously, walkers are 'voting with their feet', but anyone climbing over the spur will find a stout Arctic Circle Trail cairn,

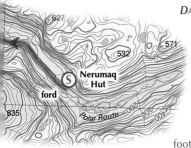

though there is no sign of a path leading to or from it. The rest of the valley is usually boggy underfoot, though there are also drier areas of willow and birch scrub. Follow the path where it exists, and, whenever it vanishes, try to locate its continuation as quickly as possible. Small streams are crossed from time to time. Steep, slabby slopes rise towards the top of Qaarajuttoq. When a lake is reached, the path runs close to the shore, or even follows its sand and gravel beaches. One in-flowing stream is rather deep, but by walking a short way upstream to pass a small, deep pool, it can be jumped across easily. The pool is often full of Arctic char.

Keep following the lake shore, but note that there is a choice of routes ahead. The shoreline path continues along the outflowing river, which quickly pours into the sea at the head of a fjord called **Kangerluarsuk Tulleq**. If this course if taken, a hut is found at the head of the fjord.

The Arctic Circle Trail, however, doesn't go to the head of the fjord, but climbs before the end of the lake.

A small river flowing into a lake can be jumped across near a pool

It isn't marked at first, but there is a narrow trodden path. Look ahead later to spot cairns, which lead across a broad crest at around 100m (330ft). Views north across the fjord take in the glaciated peaks of Aqqutikitsoq. Keep watching carefully for cairns to stay on the correct course.

A hut is seen ahead, but don't approach it directly as there is a lot of boggy ground along the way. Instead, keep straight ahead along the cairned trail until you have almost passed the hut, then turn right and walk straight towards it on a firm, dry slope. Looking along the fjord from either of the huts, other little huts will be spotted. These are all within easy reach of Sisimiut and are regularly visited by fishermen.

KANGERLUARSUK TULLEQ HUTS

◀ The hut at the head of the fjord, just above sea level, is light and spacious with a fine sea view. One large room has a sleeping platform with five mattresses, but it could accommodate up to eight people. There are a table and chairs, as well as a paraffin heater. However, the hut is often used by fishermen and may smell very strongly of fish! A couple of small rooms are used for storing all sorts of odds and ends. Bear in mind that if any local people arrive by boat, it may be possible to negotiate a passage by sea to Sisimiut.

The hill hut is located on a hump of rock around 125m (410ft) and is small and dark, with a single window. It is one small room, with a sleeping platform for three people, but three more could sleep on the floor. There is a fixed bench, a small table and a small cooking area. Water is available from a nearby stream probably fed from a snow patch in the mountains. There is no trodden path between the two huts but there is a direct line of sight and they lie 2km (1¼ miles) apart. ▶

DAY 9

Kangerluarsuk Tulleq to Sisimiut

Start	Kangerluarsuk Tulleq
Finish	Sisimiut harbour
Distance	20 or 22km (12½ or 13½ miles) depending on start point
Ascent	600 or 700m (1970 or 2295ft)
Descent	725m (2380m)
Map	Sisimiut
Terrain	After a traverse above a fjord, the route climbs through a high valley. A steep descent is followed by a gentle ascent. A final descent from the mountains gives way to a stony track and tarmac roads leading into Sisimiut.

This final day's walk is remarkably scenic, though it does experience the most changeable weather, being so close to the sea. Soggy snow patches can be a problem for anyone starting too early in the year. Most walkers will romp through the day, intent on finishing the walk and celebrating with 'real' food after so many days of eating trekking food. The busy roads of Sisimiut are a shock after spending so long in the silent wilderness. However, fond memories of the Arctic Circle Trail will endure long after trekkers are safely back home.

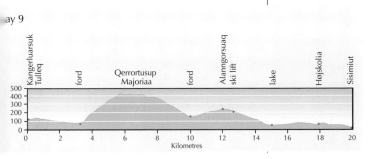

ay 9

Kangerluarsuk *it* (AS)
Tulleq
Huts
(Hut *ourist/* (S)

ford

541

574

Qerrortusup Majoriaa

Polar Route

Arctic Circle Race

001
002

400
500
600

Map continues
on page 111

If starting from the hut at the head of **Kangerluarsuk Tulleq**, then climb to the higher hut at 125m (410ft). A path can be followed from the higher hut towards a stream. The Arctic Circle Trail is joined at a cairn situated across the stream and further uphill. A narrow and continuous path traverses a slope above the fjord, but there is also a succession of little ins and outs, ups and downs. The path crosses a small rocky gully that contains a stream, then later climbs uphill, as if heading for a waterfall.

Dip a little to cross a stream below the waterfall, then continue climbing. Watch for cairns while pulling away gradually from the stream, but also watch out for a series of fine little cascades at a higher level. Looking back, the head of the fjord now looks like a lake surrounded by mountains. Further uphill, look out for a boulder perched on bare rock, but keep well to the right of it to spot more cairns. The path levels out, but is boggy underfoot for a while.

Passing through the high-level valley of Qerrortusup Majoriaa, with a view ahead of Nasaasaaq

Climb further and look for a cairn on the skyline, as well as a rather curious toilet hut. Gradients are fairly gentle as a low, rocky crest is followed, with a valley on either side. As the path enters a high-level valley at **Qerrortusup Majoriaa**, there is a long, narrow lake to the left, and a private hut can be spotted high above it. The

route touches 400m (1310ft), and snow patches may be seen nearby, even late into the summer. Views ahead reveal the serrated mountain ridge of Nasaasaaq, or Kællingehætten, framed in the valley mouth. Sisimiut is unseen, but lies beyond.

The lake ends, and the water from it drains into a flat-floored valley full of boggy moss and stony pools. Fortunately, the Arctic Circle Trail stays on firm, dry ground alongside. Walk downhill and cross a shallow, stony river. Continue through the valley, passing to the left of a little lake while heading for a gap. Pass through a strange broad, flat stony area where the river seeps in and out of shallow stony pools.

When the river begins to rush downhill towards a bouldery gorge, cross over it and climb a little, as marked by cairns. Start walking downhill in the direction of the serrated mountains. The descent is steep, then the path becomes vague on a well-vegetated slope. Look for a large boulder bearing a cairn, standing to the left of a little pool. The path continues onwards and downhill, fording a shallow stony river.

Climb gently uphill, passing to the right of a little lake, then pass to the left of a couple more little lakes. The path crosses the slopes of **Alanngorsuaq**, but watch

Looking back towards Nasaasaaq after passing the ski lift on the final descent of the trail

for a cairn ahead. Follow a low rocky ridge then step down a short, steep rocky slope. Walk towards a broad gap between Alanngorsuaq and the towering form of **Nasaasaaq**, which has permanent snow patches. Cross the rocky gap at around 250m

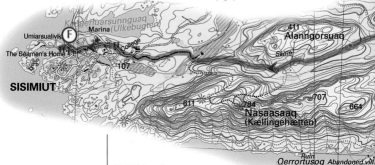

(820ft), where there might be the tiniest glimpse of the sea ahead.

Walk downhill and look to the right to spot a couple of huts and a **ski lift**. Further downhill, there is a brief view of the airport runway beyond Sisimiut, but still no view of the town. Be sure to keep to the right-hand side of the valley and later cross a stream. Climb a little, then follow a well-worn path down a boulder-studded slope. ◄

There is a sudden view of a lake, the tidal inlet of Kangerluarsunnguaq and the town of Sisimiut.

Continue down the path, then follow a dirt road along the lake shore. Walk round the end of the lake, then walk beside a patch of bog to reach a broad dirt road, which leads all the way to Sisimiut. The road rises and falls, as well as winding round low hills and hollows. Look back for fine mountain views, and listen for the barking and howling of Greenland sled dogs, tethered on the outskirts of town. Keep following the road until some blue buildings are reached, where a barrier gate gives way to a tarmac road.

Bear in mind that by climbing left here, as marked by blue-painted cairns, the Arctic Circle Trail can be linked with an ascent of Nasaasaaq (Kællingehætten).

Qerrortusúp Majoriaq

Polar Route

574
941
900
400
500
300
72
732
678

Turn left and immediately pass a bus stop on the outskirts of **Sisimiut**, to follow a road with lamp posts alongside. Keep left at a junction to follow a road with lamp posts alongside. This is Aqqusinersuaq, a main road leading straight into town, passing the Knud Rasmussenip Højskolia and Hotel Sisimiut. The least salubrious part of town has to be passed before the road serves a variety of businesses on its way to the harbour. In order not to miss anything on the way through Sisimiut, read 'Services and facilities' in the section on Sisimiut (below). Once the colourful and interesting harbour is reached, the walk along the Arctic Circle Trail can be declared over – with extra credit if you started from the ice cap!

The colourful harbour at Sisimiut

SISIMIUT

Colonial-era houses near the harbour at Sisimiut now form an interesting open-air museum

With almost 5000 years of human history behind it, Sisimiut is one of the most important towns in Greenland. It is the country's second largest town, after the capital Nuuk, with a population of about 5500. Its importance is related to its sheltered natural harbour, which remains ice-free throughout the year. Further north, harbours freeze completely in the winter months. Also, it is the southernmost town with enough snow for the pastime of dog-sledding.

At least three waves of ancient settlers are known to have reached Sisimiut, all with their roots in North America. (Sadly, an ancient settlement site near Sisimiut was destroyed to make way for a communications site.) People from the Saqqaq culture arrived 4500 years ago, and after a long tenure simply vanished. People from the Dorset culture arrived between 500BC and AD200, and also vanished. The Thule culture arrived around AD1200–1300, and its people are the ancestors of the modern Greenlandic Inuit.

The first European settlers in Greenland had little impact around Sisimiut, settling much further south. During the 1720s there were abortive attempts to set up whaling stations. One colony, known as Sydbay, or Ukiivik, was later renamed Holsteinsborg, after the missionary leader Count Johan Ludvig Holstein. In 1759 a mission-house was built at the whaling station of Asummiut. Around this time the Sydbay colony was failing, so the population transferred to the current location of Sisimiut, and in 1767 the Asummiut mission-house was dismantled and relocated there. In 1773 the Bethel Church was built, and this well-preserved blue building remains one of the most important in the colonial part of Sisimiut.

The fortunes of Sisimiut rose and fell. Smallpox decimated the population in 1801, but the pursuits of fishing and hunting provided prosperity, and the settlement recovered. Whaling later collapsed, while sealing thrived. The first fish-processing factory in Greenland was built here in 1927, along with the first shipyard in 1931. The names of Royal Greenland (fishing) and Royal Arctic (shipping) are written very prominently around the harbour.

Sisimiut's development was slow into the 1950s, but during the 1960s, when rural populations moved to the towns, there was a building boom. However, the sudden transition from rural to urban lifestyles has proved difficult for some people. In recent decades there has been a lot more emphasis on education and training for the inhabitants, along with a renewed interest in traditional arts and culture.

Today's visitor finds Sisimiut a busy and colourful place, and those who arrive there after walking the Arctic Circle Trail may take a while to adjust to the vibrancy and energy of the town. It is worth enquiring about kayak competitions at the harbour, where experienced paddlers

Jooruaqqap Aqq gives way to a path onto an interesting headland

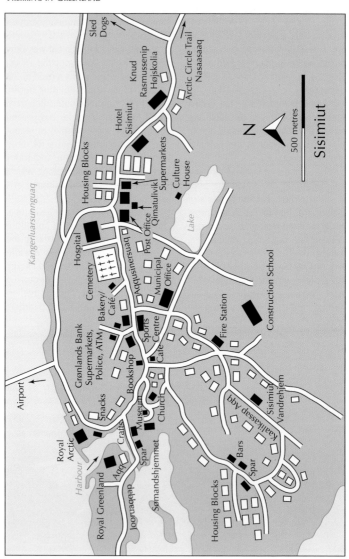

demonstrate their skills with impossibly thin and light craft.

Facilities and services

Sisimiut has an excellent range of services, and most can be found simply by following the main road, Aqqusinersuaq, straight from the Arctic Circle Trail towards the harbour. There are hotels, restaurants, bars and cafés available along or near the main road, along with supermarkets and shops.

By following the main road of Aqqusinersuaq, gently downhill from the Hotel Sisimiut, a Spar supermarket is passed before a huddle of businesses are found concentrated around a square beside the Tele-Post Centre (post office). Opening hours are Monday to Friday 1000–1700, Saturday 1000–1300. There is also a Brugseni supermarket, a sports shop and the 'Qimatulivik' building, which sells locally caught seafood, musk ox and reindeer.

Further along the road, note a cemetery full of white wooden crosses, with the Sisimiut Hospital beyond. Just after passing the cemetery, a café-bakery called J-S Tiggaliorfik lies to the right, and is the author's favourite. Shortly afterwards a sports centre lies on the left, and the road heading left at this point leads, via the fire station, to the hostel, or Sisimiut Vandrehjem.

A busy part of town features the supermarkets of Pisiffik, open daily 0700–2100, and Brugseneeraq, open Monday to Friday 0800–2400 and Saturday 1100–2400. The Politi (police station) and Grønlands Banken, open Monday to Thursday 0930–1530 and Friday 0930–1500, are also located nearby. Just a short way down the main road, the Boghandel, or bookshop, is on the right and the Café Sisimiut, specialising in Thai food, is on the left.

The main road drops steeply, with the old colonial centre and museum to the left, tel 86 25 50, www.sisimiut. museum.gl. There is a striking red church above the museum and the Sømandshjemmet offers accommodation nearby. The harbour lies straight ahead, where there is a basic snack bar and an interesting craft workshop, specialising in carved bone ornaments known as tupilaq. A Spar shop beside the harbour is usually the best place in town to obtain gas cylinders if starting the Arctic Circle Trail here.

The road called Jooruaqqap Aqq leads from the harbour towards a rugged little headland, where walkers can continue along a path to enjoy splendid views back towards the town. The path is equipped with notices explaining about historical and archaeological sites on the headland.

Hotels

Those finishing the Arctic Circle Trail pass the Hotel Sisimiut on the way into town. The hotel offers a 'hikers deal' of three nights for the price of two, which includes breakfast, one load of laundry and an hour of free wi-fi. Prices are high but it's the most comfortable place

The Sisimiut Vandrehjem offers budget accommodation

in town, offering a sauna for an additional charge. For full details and online booking, www.hotelsisimiut.com, tel 86 48 40. There is an ATM in the hotel, along with a Greenland Travel desk, while the bar-restaurant Nasaasaaq serves an extensive Greenlandic buffet, for those who wish to sample musk ox, reindeer and a range of seafood including whale and seal.

At the other end of town, above the harbour, is the Sisimiut Sømandshjemmet, or Seamen's Home. The accommodation is expensive, with wi-fi for an extra charge, although there is a reasonably priced cafeteria on site. For full details and online booking, www.soemandshjem. gl/en/hotel-sisimiut, tel 86 41 50. Profits benefit fishermen in Greenland and Denmark.

Hostel

The hostel, or Sisimiut Vandrehjem, www.sisv.dk, is open from mid-June to mid-September. It is located away from the town centre on Kaalikassap Aqq (see town plan). Please note that initial entry to the building is not normally available before 1600, until the manager is present, although residents are provided with keys on check-in. Prices start remarkably low if you choose a bunk in a shared dormitory and provide your own sleeping bag, with access to toilets, showers, self-catering kitchen and a common room. For additional payments it is possible to have a private room, bedding, towels, laundry and wi-fi access. Luggage can be stored for a few hours on the day of departure for a small fee, but not for extended periods. Although there is no longer a campsite at Sisimiut, there is room for a few tents beside the hostel, and campers can pay a small daily charge to access the facilities in the hostel. A nearby Spar shop and bars avoid the need to go all the way into the town centre for food and drink.

Transport
Bus
Blue Sisimiut Bybus services run around town, and their timetables are posted at abundant bus shelters and bus stops. There are no buses to the airport, which is 5km (3 miles) away, although it can be reached on foot in little more than one hour.

Taxi
Like the buses, these circulate around Sisimiut, as there is nowhere else to go apart from the airport. Simply flag one down or tel 86 55 33.

Ship
During the summer, a passenger ship from Nuuk berths at Sisimiut on Saturday, then heads north to Ilulissat, returning on Monday. The route is operated by Arctic Umiaq Line, tel 34 91 90, aul.gl.

Flights
Air Greenland operates flights to and from Sisimiut, offering a rapid return to Kangerlussuaq and other destinations in Greenland. Check routes, timetables and prices at www.airgreenland.com. Note that the airport is 5km (3 miles) outside town, and strong winds and fog can affect flights.

The Culture House at Sisimiut

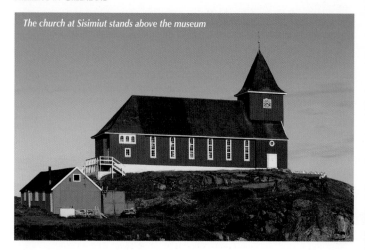
The church at Sisimiut stands above the museum

Website

Sisimiut and Kangerlussuaq are both part of the municipality of Qeqqata, whose website is available in Danish and Greenlandic at www.qeqqata. gl. The main business interests are represented by Arctic Circle Business and the main tourism interest is Destination Arctic Circle, whose website is available in English, Danish and Greenlandic, destinationarctic circle.com.

POST-AMBLE

Ascent of Nasaasaaq

Start/finish	Sisimiut
Distance	16km (10 miles) there and back
Ascent/descent	800m (2625ft)
Map	Sisimiut
Terrain	An easy track gives way to steep and stony paths, followed by even steeper rock, and a couple of lengths of fixed rope finally give access to the summit.

After walking the whole of the Arctic Circle Trail, passing fine mountains along the way, some walkers may realise that they haven't yet climbed to the top of anything! Fortunately, there is an opportunity to climb a splendid mountain at the end of the trail, directly from Sisimiut. Nasaasaaq, or Kællingehætten, towers above the town, bears permanent patches of snow, and can be reached by a popular path. However, be warned that the summit is a steep-sided rocky dome, and final access requires the use of fixed ropes.

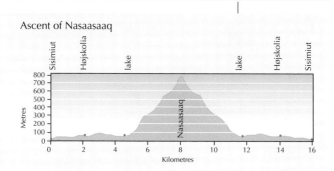

Ascent of Nasaasaaq

Start anywhere in **Sisimiut** and walk back along the main road of Aqqusinersuaq, which reaches the edge of town after passing the Hotel Sisimiut and the Knud

119

Rasmussenip Højskolia. When the road reaches a huddle
of blue buildings at a turning space, turn right to pass
a barrier gate and follow a dirt road onwards. The road
rises and falls, passing a few sled dogs before reaching
a lake. There with fine views of mountains ahead. The
ground is boggy beside the lake, but another short dirt
road runs along the shore.

Cross the bridge and keep straight ahead to pick up
a narrow path climbing left, up and across a steep rocky
slope. This is a fairly easy climb, despite the steepness of
the slope, and the path later wriggles round into a steep
little valley. Keep climbing, and note that the bedrock is
often trodden to grit, sand and dust – such is the popularity of the route.

A gap is reached at almost 300m (985ft), where
there is a path junction, and at this point blue paint
marks should have been noticed. Walking straight ahead
leads back down to the Arctic Circle Trail near the ski
lift, so turn right to continue climbing, even grappling
with bare rock for a short way. Watch for cairns and blue
paint marks, or even completely blue-painted cairns!
Whenever a choice of paths is apparent, keep to the most
well-trodden one.

The path climbs beside another valley on the
mountainside, while the gradient and terrain become gentler. There may be snow
patches here, even late into

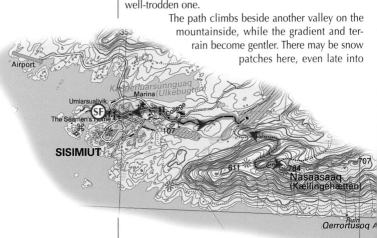

120

the summer. Looking ahead a subsidiary rocky peak is seen, rising to 611m (2005ft). The marked path is vague, but swings left up across a bouldery slope, heading away from the subsidiary peak to gain a broad crest. There is a sudden and striking view south, taking in the large islands of Maniitsorsuaq and Sarfannguit Nunataat, along with dozens of smaller islands and sundry rocks. Rising far beyond is the Sukkertoppen ice cap.

A sudden view southwards from the shoulder of Nasaasaaq reveals dozens of rugged islands

Keep left to follow the crest of the mountain, weaving between huge boulders deeply embedded in the ground. Aim for the towering rocky peak ahead and, more particularly, for a blue-painted cairn standing on top of a prominent boulder on the steep slope below the rocky peak.

Climb straight uphill as the slope becomes steeper, as well as rockier. A worn, gritty path needs care, then there are a couple of lengths of knotted ropes for protection on more exposed rock walls. Climb these, or retreat gracefully if it proves too frightening. A final scramble along a rocky ridge leads to the summit of **Nasaasaaq** at 784m (2572ft). There might still be a pole available for flying a flag!

Enjoy splendid all-round views, including those already noted to the south, as well

121

The summit of Nasaasaaq rises proudly above Sisimiut | as views back east along the Arctic Circle Trail, north to the glaciated peaks of Aqqutikitsoq, and west for a bird's-eye view of Sisimiut, to which steps should ultimately be retraced.

APPENDIX A

Route summary table

The Arctic Circle Trail between Kangerlussuaq and Sisimiut measures 165km (102½ miles). If extended to start from the ice cap, the full distance is 202km (125½ miles). Optional ascents at the start and finish total 34km (21 miles).

Stage	From/to	Distance	Ascent	Descent	Page
Preamble	Ascent of Sugar Loaf	18km (11 miles)	500m (1640ft)	500m (1640ft)	55
Optional Extension	Ice Cap to Kangerlussuaq	37km (23 miles) or 25km (15½ miles)	340m (1115ft) or 240m (785ft)	1000m (3280ft) or 700m (2295ft)	58
1	Kangerlussuaq to Hundeso	20km (12½ miles)	505m (1655ft)	335m (1100ft)	65
2	Hundeso to Katifik	20km (12½ miles)	470m (1540ft)	520m (1705ft)	71
3	Katifik to Canoe Centre	20km (12½ miles)	200m (665ft)	200m (665ft)	76
4	Canoe Centre to Ikkattooq	22km (13½ miles)	650m (2130ft)	450m (1475ft)	82
5	Ikkattooq to Eqalugaarniarfik	11km (7 miles)	330m (1080ft)	520m (1705ft)	87
6	Eqalugaarniarfik to Innajuattoq	19km (12 miles)	680m (2230ft)	510m (1675ft)	93
7	Innajuattoq to Nerumaq	17km (10½ miles)	370m (1215ft)	520m (1705ft)	98
8	Nerumaq to Kangerluarsuk Tulleq	17km (10½ miles)	300m (985ft)	325m (1065ft)	102
9	Kangerluarsuk Tulleq to Sisimiut	20km (12½ miles)	700m (2295ft)	725m (2380ft)	107
Post-amble	Ascent of Nasaasaaq	16km (10 miles)	800m (2625ft)	800m (2625ft)	119

APPENDIX B

Language notes and glossary

Greenlandic is the native language of Greenland. West Greenlandic, or Kalaallisut, is spoken at either end of the Arctic Circle Trail. It is courteous to be able to speak a few words of Greenlandic, but anything more gets quite complicated. Written words run together, so that a whole sentence might become a single word, and the spoken word is very soft and difficult to pronounce. Danish, the colonial language, is widely spoken and is taught alongside Greenlandic in schools, so it can be helpful to know a little of it. Many people working regularly with tourists speak English.

English	Danish	Greenlandic
Pleasantries		
Hello	Goddag	*Kutaa*
Goodbye	Farvel	*Baaj*
Please	Værsgo	*Takanna*
Thank you	Tak	*Qujanaq*
Yes	Ja	*Aap*
No	Nej	*Naagga*
Maybe	Måske	*Immaqa*
My name is ...	Jeg hedder ...	*... mik ateqarpunga*
What's your name?	Hvad hedder du?	*Qanoq ateqarpit?*
Directions		
North	Nord	*Avannaa*
South	Syd	*Kujataa*
East	Øst	*Kangia*
West	Vest	*Kitaa*
Right	Højre	*Talerpik*
Left	Venstre	*Saamik*
Where is the ...?	Hvor er ...?	*Sumiippa ...?*
Campsite	Campingpladsen	*Tutertarfimmut*
Hut	Hytte	*Illuluk*
Youth hostel	Vandrehjem	*Angalaartut*
Hotel	Hotel	*Hotelimut*
Tourist office	Turistbureauet	*Turistit allaffiannut*
Post office	Postkontoret	*Allakkerivimmut*

English	Danish	Greenlandic
Shop	Butik	*Pisiniarfik*
Police station	Politiet	*Politeeqarfimmut*
Airport	Lufthavn	*Timmisartoqarfimmut*
Harbour	Havnen	*Umiarsualiviup*
Canoe	Kano	*Qajaq (Anglicised as 'kayak')*
Midge net	Myggenet	*Ippernaaqqut*
Money Matters		
Credit card	Kreditkort	*Akiliissut*
Money	Penge	*Akissaq*
Food and Drink		
Apple	Æble	*Iipili*
Beer	Øl	*Immiaq*
Bread	Brød	*Iffiaq*
Breakfast	Morgenmad	*Ullaakkorsiut*
Chicken	Kylling	*Kukkukuuaraq*
Chocolate	Chokolade	*Sukkulaa*
Coffee	Kaffe	*Kaffi*
Dessert	Dessert	*Kinguleraq*
Dried fruit	Tørret frugt	*Pupiusat*
Drink	Drik	*Imigassaq*
Egg	Æg	*Mannik*
Fruit	Frugt	*Inerititaq*
Greenlandic food	Grønlandsk mad	*Kalaalimernit*
Halibut	Hellefisk	*Qaleralik*
Ham	Skinke	*Nallu*
Milk	Mælk	*Millek*
Mussels	Muslinger	*Uillut*
Open sandwich	Smørrebrød	*Qallersukkat*
Orange	Appelsin	*Appelsiina*
Potato	Kartoffler	*Issuusaq*
Rice	Ris	*Suaasat*
Sausage	Pølse	*Immigaq*
Shrimp	Rejer	*Raajat*
Soda	Sodavand	*Sodavandi*
Tea	Te	*Tii*
Vegetables	Grønsager	*Naatiiat*
Water	Vand	*Imeq*

English	Danish	Greenlandic
Whale meat	Hvalkød	*Tikaanguliup neqaa*
Wine	Vin	*Viinni*
Wildlife		
Bird	Fugl	*Timmiaq*
Dog	Hund	*Qimmeq*
Eagle	Ørn	*Nattoralik*
Fox	Ræv	*Terrianiaq*
Hare	Hare	*Ukaleq*
Midge	Myg	*Ippernaq*
Musk ox	Moskusokse	*Ummimaq*
Polar bear	Isbjørn	*Nanoq (Anglicised as 'nanook')*
Reindeer	Rensdyr	*Tuttu*
Seal	Sæl	*Puisi*
Whale	Hval	*Arfeq*
Days of the week		
Sunday	Søndag	*Sapaat*
Monday	Mandag	*Ataasinngorneq*
Tuesday	Tirsdag	*Marlunngorneq*
Wednesday	Onsdag	*Pingasunngorneq*
Thursday	Torsdag	*Sisamanngorneq*
Friday	Fredag	*Tallimanngorneq*
Saturday	Lørdag	*Arfininngorneq*
Numbers		
One	En/Et	*Ataaseq*
Two	To	*Marluk*
Three	Tre	*Pingasut*
Four	Fire	*Sisamat*
Five	Fem	*Tallimat*
Six	Seks	*Arfinillit*
Seven	Syv	*Arfineq marluk*
Eight	Otte	*Arfineq pingasut*
Nine	Ni	*Qulaaluat*
Ten	Ti	*Qulit*
Eleven	Elleve	*Aqqanillit*
Twelve	Tolv	*Aqqaneq marluk*

There are no Greenlandic numbers beyond 12, so Danish numbers must be used.

English	Danish	Greenlandic
When all else fails		
Help!	Hjælp!	*Ikiunnga!*
I don't understand	Jeg forstar ikke	*Passinngilara*
Do you speak English?	Taler du engelsk?	*Engelsk oqaluttarpit?*
Topographical Glossary		
Arctic Circle	Nordlige Polarkreds	*Qaasuitsup Killeqarfia Avannarleq*
Big lake	Stor sø	*Tasersuaq*
Black	Sort	*Qernertoq*
Blue	Blå	*Tungujortoq*
Brown	Brun	*Sukkulaajusaq*
Fjord	Fiord	*Kangerluk*
Glacier	Gletsjer	*Sermertaq*
Green	Grøn	*Qorsuk*
Greenland	Grønland	*Kalaallit Nunaannut*
Grey	Grå	*Qasersoq*
Headland	Forbjerg	*Nuuk*
Iceberg	Isbjerge	*Ilulissat*
Ice cap	Inlandsisen	*Sermerssuaq*
Island	Ø	*Qeqertaq*
Lake	Sø	*Taseq*
Mountain	Bjerg	*Qaqaq*
Peninsula	Halbinsel	*Qeqertaaminerssua*
Red	Rød	*Aapaluttoq*
River	Elv	*Kuuk*
Valley	Dal	*Qooroq*
West Greenland	Vestgrønland	*Kitaa*
White	Hvid	*Qaqortoq*
Yellow	Gul	*Katortoq*

APPENDIX C
Useful contacts

TOURISM

If spending any time exploring in Copenhagen, see www.copenhagen.com. A good portal for tourism in Greenland is www.visitgreenland.com. There is also an Arctic Circle Trail Facebook group at www.facebook.com/groups/arcticcircletrail. Numerous blogs and online accounts of the trail are available, but one that is definitely worth reading is Bo Normander's at www.greenlandicseasons.dk/en/arctic-circle-trail.

LOCAL INFORMATION

Sisimiut and Kangerlussuaq are both part of the municipality of Qeqqata, whose website is available in Danish and Greenlandic at wwww.qeqqata.gl. The main business interests are represented by Arctic Circle Business and the main tourism interest is Destination Arctic Circle, whose website is available in English, Danish and Greenlandic, destinationarcticcircle.com. The official website for the Arctic Circle Trail is arcticcircletrail.gl.

MUSEUMS

Kangerlussuaq Museum, tel 84 13 00. Sisimiut Museum, tel 85 25 50, www.sisimiut.museum.gl.

TOUR OPERATORS

Albatros Arctic Circle is based at Polar Lodge in Kangerlussuaq, tel 84 10 16, albatros-arctic-circle.com. Kang Mini Tours is based in Kangerlussuaq, tel 51 01 07, www.kangtours.dk.
Greenland Travel has a desk at the Sisimiut Hotel, tel 86 75 30, www.greenland-travel.com. Most accommodation providers will know of opportunities for additional tours.

ARCTIC CIRCLE TRAIL MAPS

Three 'Hiking Maps' cover the trail, published by Greenland Tourism, at a scale of 1:100,000. The relevant sheets are 'Kangerlussuaq', 'Pingu' and 'Sisimiut'. Buy them in advance of travel if possible, though they are on sale in Kangerlussuaq and Sisimiut. Stockists include Harvey Map Services, 12–22 Main Street, Doune, FK16 6BJ, tel 01786 841202, www.harveymaps.co.uk; Stanfords, 7 Mercer Walk, Covent Garden, London, WC2H 9FA, tel 020 78361321, www.stanfords.co.uk; The Map Shop, 15 High Street, Upton upon Severn, Worcestershire, WR8 0HJ, tel 01684

593146, www.themapshop.co.uk; and Cordee, www.cordee.co.uk. The maps are also available for use on GPS enabled devices through the Avenza Maps app.

Saga Maps, www.sagamaps.com, publish a single 1:25,000 sheet covering this part of Greenland, but it lacks detail and does not show the course of the Arctic Circle Trail. However, Sheet number 8, 'Sisimiut Kangerlussuaq', offers a useful overview of the whole area between the ice cap and the coast.

Arctic Sun Maps produce a 'Kangerlussuaq-Sisimiut' sheet at a scale of 1:250,000, showing the Arctic Circle Trail. There is also a 'Kangerlussuaq' map at a scale of 1:50,000. See arcticsunmaps.weebly.com or look out for them once in Greenland.

TRAVEL AND TRANSPORT
To Copenhagen
By air
Every country in Europe and several cities in Britain have direct flights to Copenhagen. Most are operated by Scandinavian Airlines (SAS), www.flysas. com, but others include Norwegian, www.norwegian.com; British Airways, www.britishairways.com; and EasyJet, www.easyjet.com. SAS also has direct flights to Copenhagen from Chicago, New York (Newark) and Washington DC.

By train
From Britain, via the Channel Tunnel, France, Belgium and Germany, check options with the 'Man in Seat 61', www.seat61.com.

By coach
From London to Brussels and Brussels to Copenhagen, using Eurolines coaches, www.eurolines.com.

To Greenland
Flights
Flights from Copenhagen to Kangerlussuaq, and between Kangerlussuaq and Sisimiut, are operated by Air Greenland. They have offices at the airport at Kangerlussuaq, tel 84 11 42, www.airgreenland.com.

Local transport
Buses
The Kangerlussuaq Bybus and Sisimiut Bybus provide regular town services at either end of the Arctic Circle Trail. There are abundant bus shelters and bus stops where timetables are posted. Towns and villages in Greenland do not have bus links with each other as there are rarely any roads linking them.

Taxis

For taxis around Kangerlussuaq, tel 56 56 56. For taxis around Sisimiut, tel 86 55 33.

Ships

The harbour near Kangerlussuaq is served only by cruise ships. The harbour at Sisimiut is visited by a ship on Saturday, which proceeds to Ilulissat, returning on Monday to sail to Nuuk. This is operated by Arctic Umiaq Line, tel 34 91 90, aul.gl.

LANGUAGE

Most online translation websites help with English/Danish translations. For English/Danish/Greenlandic translation, see oqaasileriffik.gl.

STOVE FUEL

Fuel cannot be carried on flights to Greenland, but can be purchased in Kangerlussuaq and Sisimiut. A variety of pierceable and resealable gas canisters are available. Flammable liquids include methylated spirit (*husholdnings sprit*), paraffin or kerosene (*lampeolie*), and petroleum, white gas or naphtha (*benzin*). These are all bottled by Borup, www.borupkemi.dk. Instructions for the safe operation of the 'Refleks' paraffin heaters in most of the huts along the trail can be obtained from www.refleks-olieovne.dk.

ARCTIC CIRCLE EVENTS

The Polar Circle Marathon takes place over a single day in October, between the ice cap and Kangerlussuaq. Details at www.polar-circle-marathon.com. The Arctic Circle Race is a skiing event that takes place over three days in March from Sisimiut. Details at www.acr.gl.

GUIDED WALKS

Most walkers on the Arctic Circle Trail are completely self-sufficient. However, there are very occasional opportunities to join or organise a guided walk along the trail, using the knowledge and expertise of people who know the trail. Check the Arctic Circle Trail trips organised by Mike Laing of Snowdonia Climbing, www.snowdoniaclimbing.co.uk.

COMMUNICATIONS

The country code for Greenland is +299 and there are no area codes. Inside Greenland, simply dial the six-figure telephone number. Bear in mind that telephones and signals for mobile phones are only available in Kangerlussuaq and Sisimiut. Most providers have no roaming agreements with Greenland. Satellite phones can be carried on the trail, but only take them after being instructed in their correct use.

EMERGENCY CONTACTS

For mountain/wilderness rescue in Greenland, the first point of contact is the police (politi). Ring Sisimiut, tel 70 13 22, or 70 14 48 in the evenings; or Kangerlussuaq, tel 70 13 24 or 70 14 48 in the evenings. In case of illness or injury there is a hospital at Sisimiut, tel 86 42 11, and a nursing station at Kangerlussuaq Airport, tel 86 88 12.

Colourful buildings reflect in the sea water at the head of the narrow natural harbour at Sisimiut

DOWNLOAD THE ROUTES
IN GPX FORMAT

All the routes in this guide are available for download from:

www.cicerone.co.uk/967/GPX

as standard format GPX files. You should be able to load them into most online GPX systems and mobile devices, whether GPS or smartphone. You may need to convert the file into your preferred format using a conversion programme such as gpsvisualizer.com or one of the many other such websites and programmes.

When you follow this link, you will be asked for your email address and where you purchased the guidebook, and have the option to subscribe to the Cicerone e-newsletter.

www.cicerone.co.uk

LISTING OF CICERONE GUIDES

BRITISH ISLES CHALLENGES, COLLECTIONS AND ACTIVITIES

Cycling Land's End to John o' Groats
Great Walks on the England
  Coast Path
The Big Rounds
The Book of the Bivvy
The Book of the Bothy
The Mountains of England & Wales:
  Vol 1 Wales
  Vol 2 England
The National Trails
Walking The End to End Trail

SCOTLAND

Ben Nevis and Glen Coe
Cycle Touring in Northern Scotland
Cycling in the Hebrides
Great Mountain Days in Scotland
Mountain Biking in Southern
  and Central Scotland
Mountain Biking in West and
  North West Scotland
Not the West Highland Way
  Scotland
Scotland's Mountain Ridges
Scottish Wild Country Backpacking
Skye's Cuillin Ridge Traverse
The Borders Abbeys Way
The Great Glen Way
The Great Glen Way Map Booklet
The Hebridean Way
The Hebrides
The Isle of Mull
The Isle of Skye
The Skye Trail
The Southern Upland Way
The Speyside Way
The Speyside Way Map Booklet
The West Highland Way
The West Highland Way
  Map Booklet
Walking Ben Lawers,
  Rannoch and Atholl
Walking in the Cairngorms
Walking in the Pentland Hills
Walking in the Scottish Borders
Walking in the Southern Uplands
Walking in Torridon, Fisherfield,
  Fannichs and An Teallach
Walking Loch Lomond and
  the Trossachs
Walking on Arran
Walking on Harris and Lewis
Walking on Jura, Islay and Colonsay
Walking on Rum and the Small Isles
Walking on the Orkney and
  Shetland Isles
Walking on Uist and Barra
Walking the Cape Wrath Trail

Walking the Corbetts
  Vol 1 South of the Great Glen
  Vol 2 North of the Great Glen
Walking the Galloway Hills
Walking the Munros
  Vol 1 – Southern, Central
  and Western Highlands
  Vol 2 – Northern Highlands
  and the Cairngorms
Winter Climbs Ben Nevis
  and Glen Coe

NORTHERN ENGLAND ROUTES

Cycling the Reivers Route
Cycling the Way of the Roses
Hadrian's Cycleway
Hadrian's Wall Path
Hadrian's Wall Path Map Booklet
The C2C Cycle Route
The Coast to Coast Map Booklet
The Coast to Coast Walk
The Pennine Way
The Pennine Way Map Booklet
Walking the Dales Way
Walking the Dales Way
  Map Booklet

NORTH-EAST ENGLAND, YORKSHIRE DALES AND PENNINES

Cycling in the Yorkshire Dales
Great Mountain Days in
  the Pennines
Mountain Biking in the
  Yorkshire Dales
St Oswald's Way and
  St Cuthbert's Way
The Cleveland Way and the
  Yorkshire Wolds Way
The Cleveland Way Map Booklet
The North York Moors
The Reivers Way
Trail and Fell Running in
  the Yorkshire Dales
Walking in County Durham
Walking in Northumberland
Walking in the North Pennines
Walking in the Yorkshire
  Dales: North and East
Walking in the Yorkshire
  Dales: South and West

NORTH-WEST ENGLAND AND THE ISLE OF MAN

Cycling the Pennine Bridleway
Isle of Man Coastal Path
The Lancashire Cycleway
The Lune Valley and Howgills
Walking in Cumbria's Eden Valley
Walking in Lancashire

Walking in the Forest of
  Bowland and Pendle
Walking on the Isle of Man
Walking on the West
  Pennine Moors
Walks in Silverdale and Arnside

LAKE DISTRICT

Cycling in the Lake District
Great Mountain Days in the
  Lake District
Joss Naylor's Lakes, Meres and
  Waters of the Lake District
Lake District Winter Climbs
Lake District: High Level and
  Fell Walks
Lake District: Low Level and
  Lake Walks
Mountain Biking in the Lake District
Outdoor Adventures with
  Children – Lake District
Scrambles in the Lake
  District – North
Scrambles in the Lake
  District – South
Trail and Fell Running in the
  Lake District
Walking The Cumbria Way
Walking the Lake District Fells –
  Borrowdale
  Buttermere
  Coniston
  Keswick
  Langdale
  Mardale and the Far East
  Patterdale
  Wasdale
Walking the Tour of the
  Lake District

DERBYSHIRE, PEAK DISTRICT AND MIDLANDS

Cycling in the Peak District
Dark Peak Walks
Scrambles in the Dark Peak
Walking in Derbyshire
Walking in the Peak District –
  White Peak East
Walking in the Peak District –
  White Peak West

SOUTHERN ENGLAND

20 Classic Sportive Rides
  in South East England
20 Classic Sportive Rides
  in South West England
Cycling in the Cotswolds
Mountain Biking on the
  North Downs
Mountain Biking on the
  South Downs

Suffolk Coast and Heath Walks
The Cotswold Way
The Cotswold Way Map Booklet
The Kennet and Avon Canal
The Lea Valley Walk
The North Downs Way
The North Downs Way
   Map Booklet
The Peddars Way and
   Norfolk Coast Path
The Pilgrims' Way
The Ridgeway National Trail
The Ridgeway Map Booklet
The South Downs Way
The South Downs Way Map Booklet
The Thames Path
The Thames Path Map Booklet
The Two Moors Way
The Two Moors Way Map Booklet
Walking Hampshire's Test Way
Walking in Cornwall
Walking in Essex
Walking in Kent
Walking in London
Walking in Norfolk
Walking in the Chilterns
Walking in the Cotswolds
Walking in the Isles of Scilly
Walking in the New Forest
Walking in the North
   Wessex Downs
Walking on Dartmoor
Walking on Guernsey
Walking on Jersey
Walking on the Isle of Wight
Walking the Jurassic Coast
Walking the South West Coast Path
Walking the South West Coast Path
   Map Booklets
   Vol 1: Minehead to St Ives
   Vol 2: St Ives to Plymouth
   Vol 3: Plymouth to Poole
Walks in the South Downs
   National Park

WALES AND WELSH BORDERS

Cycle Touring in Wales
Cycling Lon Las Cymru
Glyndwr's Way
Great Mountain Days in Snowdonia
Hillwalking in Shropshire
Hillwalking in Wales – Vols 1&2
Mountain Walking in Snowdonia
Offa's Dyke Path
Offa's Dyke Path Map Booklet
Ridges of Snowdonia
Scrambles in Snowdonia
Snowdonia: 30 Low-level and
   Easy Walks – North
Snowdonia: 30 Low-level and
   Easy Walks – South
The Cambrian Way

The Ceredigion and
   Snowdonia Coast Paths
The Pembrokeshire Coast Path
The Pembrokeshire Coast Path
   Map Booklet
The Severn Way
The Snowdonia Way
The Wye Valley Walk
Walking in Carmarthenshire
Walking in Pembrokeshire
Walking in the Brecon Beacons
Walking in the Forest of Dean
Walking in the Wye Valley
Walking on Gower
Walking the Shropshire Way
Walking the Wales Coast Path

INTERNATIONAL CHALLENGES, COLLECTIONS AND ACTIVITIES

Europe's High Points

AFRICA

Kilimanjaro
Walks and Scrambles in the
   Moroccan Anti-Atlas
Walking in the Drakensberg

ALPS CROSS-BORDER ROUTES

100 Hut Walks in the Alps
Alpine Ski Mountaineering
   Vol 1 – Western Alps
   Vol 2 – Central and Eastern Alps
The Karnischer Hohenweg
The Tour of the Bernina
Trail Running – Chamonix and
   the Mont Blanc region
Trekking Chamonix to Zermatt
Trekking in the Alps
Trekking in the Silvretta and
   Ratikon Alps
Trekking Munich to Venice
Trekking the Tour of Mont Blanc
Walking in the Alps

PYRENEES AND FRANCE/SPAIN CROSS-BORDER ROUTES

Shorter Treks in the Pyrenees
The GR10 Trail
The GR11 Trail
The Pyrenean Haute Route
The Pyrenees
Walks and Climbs in the Pyrenees

AUSTRIA

Innsbruck Mountain Adventures
Trekking in Austria's Hohe Tauern
Trekking in the Stubai Alps
Trekking in the Zillertal Alps
Walking in Austria
Walking in the Salzkammergut:
   the Austrian Lake District

EASTERN EUROPE

The Danube Cycleway Vol 2
The Elbe Cycle Route
The High Tatras
The Mountains of Romania
Walking in Bulgaria's National Parks
Walking in Hungary

FRANCE, BELGIUM AND LUXEMBOURG

Camino de Santiago – Via Podiensis
Chamonix Mountain Adventures
Cycle Touring in France
Cycling London to Paris
Cycling the Canal de la Garonne
Cycling the Canal du Midi
Cycling the Route des
   Grandes Alpes
Mont Blanc Walks
Mountain Adventures in
   the Maurienne
Short Treks on Corsica
The GR5 Trail
The GR5 Trail – Benelux
   and Lorraine
The GR5 Trail – Vosges and Jura
The Grand Traverse of the
   Massif Central
The Moselle Cycle Route
The River Loire Cycle Route
Trekking in the Vanoise
Trekking the Cathar Way
Trekking the GR20 Corsica
Trekking the Robert Louis
   Stevenson Trail
Via Ferratas of the French Alps
Walking in Provence – East
Walking in Provence – West
Walking in the Ardennes
Walking in the Auvergne
Walking in the Briançonnais
Walking in the Dordogne
Walking in the Haute Savoie: North
Walking in the Haute Savoie: South
Walking on Corsica
Walking the Brittany Coast Path

GERMANY

Hiking and Cycling in the
   Black Forest
The Danube Cycleway Vol 1
The Rhine Cycle Route
The Westweg
Walking in the Bavarian Alps

IRELAND

The Wild Atlantic Way and
   Western Ireland
Walking the Wicklow Way

For full information on all our guides, books and eBooks, visit our website:
www.cicerone.co.uk

CICERONE

Trust Cicerone to guide your next adventure, wherever it may be around the world...

Discover guides for hiking, mountain walking, backpacking, trekking, trail running, cycling and mountain biking, ski touring, climbing and scrambling in Britain, Europe and worldwide.

Connect with Cicerone online and find inspiration.

- buy books and ebooks
- articles, advice and trip reports
- podcasts and live events
- GPX files and updates
- regular newsletter

cicerone.co.uk